T0396285

My BIG book of Phonics

Contents

Introduction

Welcome to *My Big Book of Phonics*—a one-stop introduction to first phonic sounds and vocabulary that you and your child will want to look at again and again.

Reading is one of the most important things we can teach children. Reading allows a child to "lift words from the page" to access exciting stories, wonderful poems and fascinating facts. Becoming a good reader sets them up for success throughout their school life and on into adulthood. Learning phonics is the foundation of becoming a good reader and is the approach taken to teach reading and writing for children aged 4 to 7. Packed with illustrations and simple explanations, this book introduces all the key sounds, letters, and concepts your child will need to learn about phonics.

But first, let's think about how written language is put together.

Cracking the code

Writing is like a code that uses the letters of the alphabet to represent the sounds we say in spoken words. For example, in the word "sun" there are three sounds /s/ /u/ /n/ represented by the letters **s**, **u**, and **n**. When we read the word "sun," we use our knowledge of the code to recall the sounds /s/ /u/ /n/ in order and then blend them or "push them together" to get the word. Blending sounds is a key skill that children learn alongside the code.

Notice that sounds are written within forward slashes, for example /a/ and /f/, to distinguish them from letters.

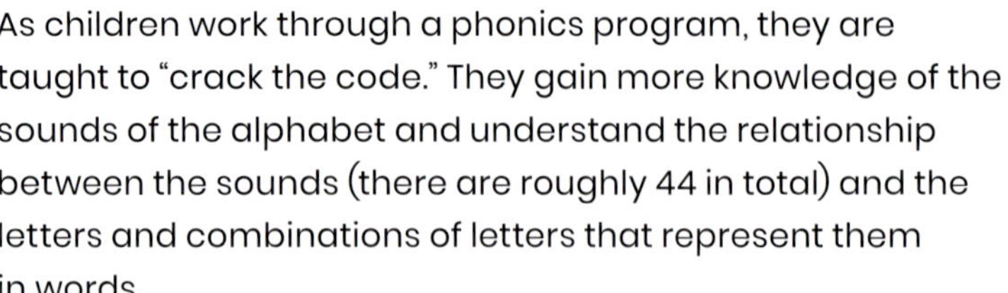

As children work through a phonics program, they are taught to "crack the code." They gain more knowledge of the sounds of the alphabet and understand the relationship between the sounds (there are roughly 44 in total) and the letters and combinations of letters that represent them in words.

Phonics programs start with the simplest parts of the code, with letters and sounds introduced according to how common they are in English (rather than in alphabetical order). As children move through a program, they learn about the more complicated aspects of the code. For example, some sounds are represented by more than one letter working together. As a child's knowledge and skill grows,their reading becomes more accurate and fluent.

My Big Book of Phonics takes this same approach so you and your child can gradually explore the sounds of the alphabet together.

Exploring the sounds

At the start of a phonics program, children are given the impression that each sound is represented by just a single letter. This stage is often described as basic or **initial code**. This is an opportunity to focus on teaching the important skill of blending in simple words, while building the child's confidence *(see pages 12–55)*.

Children begin by "sounding out" simple three-letter words, made up of a consonant, a vowel, and a consonant (referred to as **CVC words**). These are words such as "sit" and "run." Words that have two consonants next to each other are more difficult for children because blending adjacent consonants is trickier than blending a vowel and consonant. Programs make time for children to practice working with these types of words, gradually increasing the difficulty. For example, they move on to words such as "fast," "frog," and "stand" *(see pages 56–64 and 72–76)*.

Once children move on from the initial stage, they learn that some sounds are represented by more than one letter "working together." For example, in the word "tell" the /l/ sound is represented by two letters: **ll**. **Graphemes** (combinations of letters) with two letters in them are called **digraphs**. Graphemes with three letters in them, such as **are** representing the sound /air/ in the word "fare," are called **trigraphs** and graphemes with four letters in them are called **tetragraphs** *(see pages 66–71 and 120–31)*.

Children are now ready to tackle advanced or extended code. At this stage, they learn that some sounds are represented by more than one grapheme. For example, the /oa/ sound is represented by **oa**, **oe**, **ow**, **o**, and **o_e** in the words "boat," "toe," "snow," "no," and "joke," *(see pages 86 onward)*.

Soon children are ready to tackle much longer words. When we say long words, we naturally group sounds together in chunks, which we say in "beats," or in a rhythm. These chunks are called **syllables**, and identifying them can help a child with reading and spelling. When we say these words, we often say an "uh" sound in place of the regular sound pattern to make the flow of speaking easier. For example, in the word kitten the /e/ sound is spoken as an "uh" sound. This is surprisingly common, and this sound is given the name **schwa** *(see page 118)*.

When the child's reading is really getting going, it's helpful to introduce some simple word endings or **suffixes** so they can read a wider range of books and texts. Check out pages 132–5 to look at some common endings that change the function of words or relate to plurals. Note that the endings **-ing**, **-es**, **-ies**, and **-ly** are made up of more than one sound.

So, that's phonics in a nutshell!

> **"Cracking the code" is the strong foundation on which good readers and spellers are built.**

Over time, a child will develop increasing accuracy and fluency, calling upon their phonics knowledge all the while. Enjoy exploring the code with your child.

Your child's phonics program

Not all phonics programs are the same. Different programs have different teaching orders of sounds, and they also differ in their approach to some aspects of the code. It's important to be aware of the teaching order of the program your child's school uses.

Some programs teach children the technical terms **phoneme** for sound and **grapheme** for letter (or combination of letters), so the child may be aware of and use these.

Your child's program may describe vowels as either short or long. **Short vowels** are generally shorter in duration when spoken, e.g., /a/ and /o/, while **long vowels** are generally longer in duration when spoken, e.g., /ee/ /ai/ and /oo/. If your child is taught this, then it is helpful to refer to these when using the book. Some programs do not refer to these terms at all and instead concentrate on the simple principle that letters represent sounds.

In some programs, some letters are described as **silent**. For example, in the word "knight" the **k** is silent. Another way of looking at this is that the letters **kn** together represent the sound /n/.

Whichever approach your school's program takes, it is helpful to use the same approach at home.

How to use this book

You can use *My Big Book of Phonics* in lots of different ways to explore the code with your child. Your support will help them to remember the sounds and graphemes they are learning as they begin their reading journey at school or at home.

You might dip in and out of the book to support what your child is learning in their phonics program at school or find out about the sounds and letters you and your child encounter when you are sharing books together. Alternatively, your child might simply enjoy browsing the pages, spotting pictures, letters, and words, all the while learning lots about phonics.

As a starting point, the book presents the child with an illustrated scene or series of pictures that relate to a grapheme and sound focus. On most pages the focus will be a grapheme (a letter or a combination of letters that represent a sound). The illustrated scene is visually appealing, of course, but there is much more to it than that.

Children can point to and say aloud words containing the target sound to help them commit it to memory. You can prompt them using the answers section on the page. Talking about the scene also supports the development of a wider vocabulary, which is important for reading comprehension. Widening a child's vocabulary now will support their reading in the long term as they encounter a broader range of words when they begin to read independently.

If you want to find out about a particular grapheme, sound, or group of sounds, refer to the contents page *(see pages 2–3)*, which will guide you to the relevant pages. The sound charts *(see pages 8–11)* are also a handy reference as they show the bigger picture of how the sounds are represented.

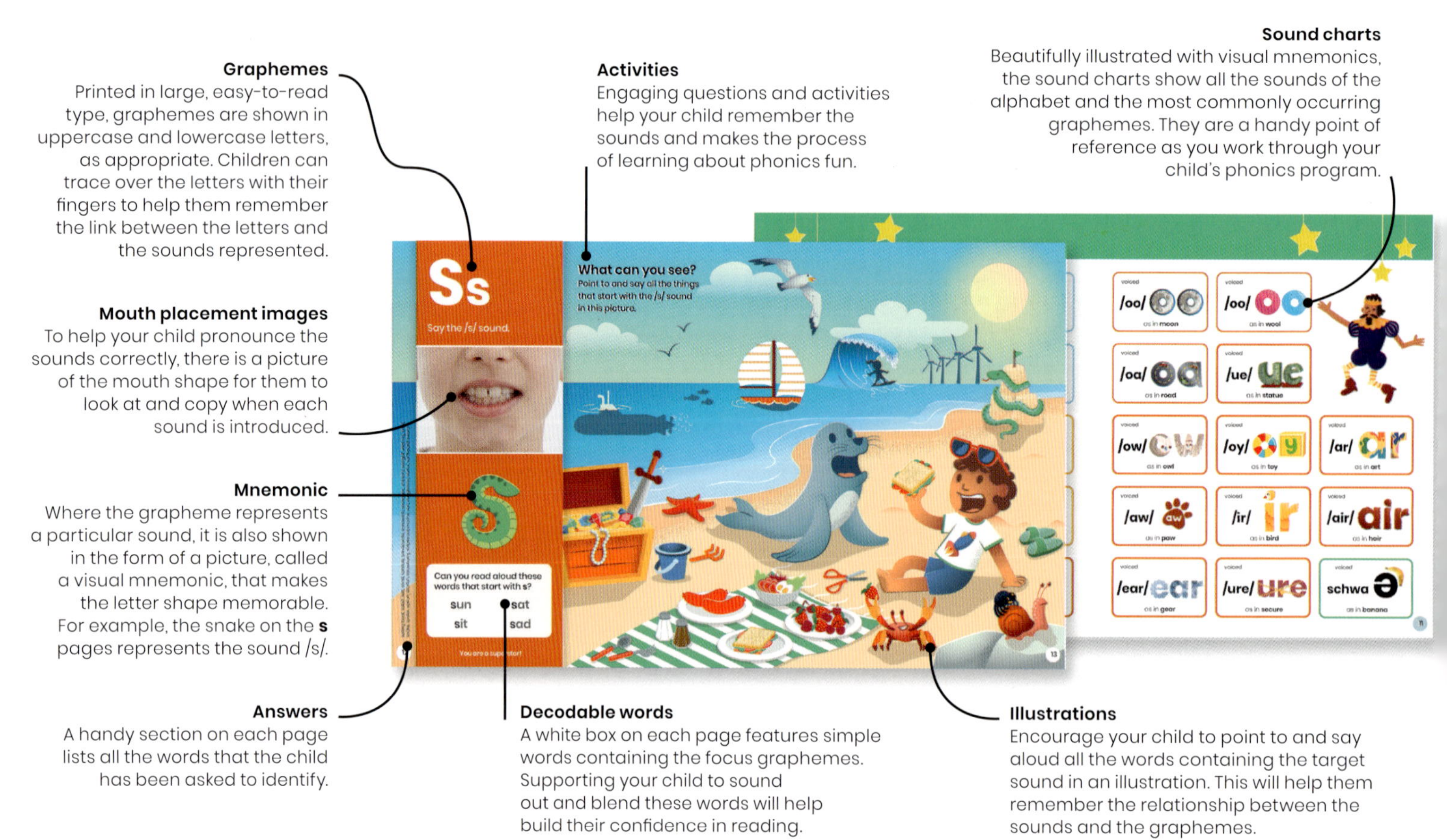

Suggested activities

- Think about each sound and encourage your child to say it clearly. Look at the picture of the mouth shape and ask your child to check in a mirror that their mouth is making the same shape. Can they think of any more words that start with that sound or (later in the book) have that sound in them?

- Focus on the pictures in the scene. Encourage your child to say what each picture is and say whether or not it starts with the sound. Play "I Spy" or count how many pictures they can find that start with the sound. Can they find more than you? Together make up some silly sentences containing the words and have fun with them. For example, "A sneaky seal snatched Sam's sausage sandwich! Think about expanding their vocabulary!

- Focus on the scene. Talk about the scene together and recall any experiences you have had related to what you can see.

- Look at the focus grapheme and ask your child to trace over it with their finger, saying the matching sound at the same time. Always connect the grapheme to the sound. Whenever your child writes the grapheme, have them say the sound at the same time. If they need some help, step in and say the sound for them. They can try writing it in the air (as big as they can), or, if you don't mind getting messy, in shaving cream or rice. Offer a choice of writing tools, such as different thicknesses of pens and pencils, crayons, paint, sponges, or fingers, and write on different media, such as paper, cardboard, whiteboard, blackboard, or even sandpaper.

- Focus on the words. Support your child in reading the words using their code knowledge and blending the sounds together. Help out as they need. Make up a simple sentence with one of the words in. Write it on a piece of paper but miss out the word and ask your child to write the word in, saying the sounds as they write each grapheme. Read back the sentence, with your child following along, joining in when you get to the word they can read.

- Can your child find in the book the grapheme and sound that starts their name, or the name of their friends or pets?

- Ask your child to trace one of the graphemes on your back and try to guess the sound. Swap and see if your child can work out what the sound is from the grapheme.

- At a later stage, can your child find three graphemes that represent a target sound, for example, finding words containing the sound /ai/ – **ay**, as in "play," ai, as in "train," or a, as in "baby"?

Explore the code, learn about the sounds and letters, and have fun! Enjoy your child's journey to reading and spelling success with phonics as a firm foundation.

Sound charts

In the tiles below, the main sounds of the English language are represented using visual mnemonics featuring commonly occurring graphemes. The chart is color coded, to show the types of graphemes children may encounter in their phonics programs, and specifies if a sound is voiced or unvoiced (*see page 143*).

Key

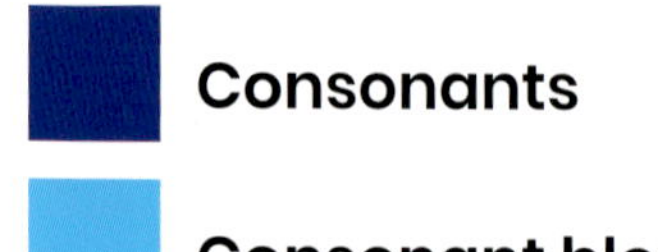

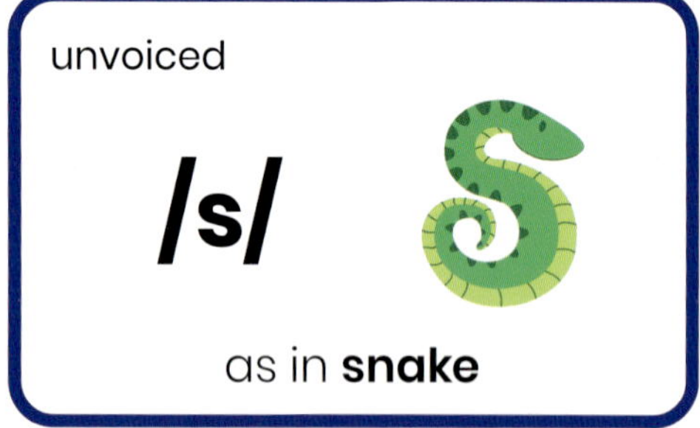

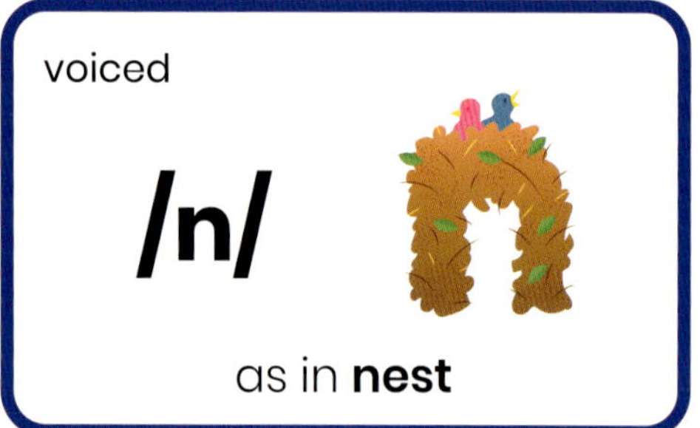

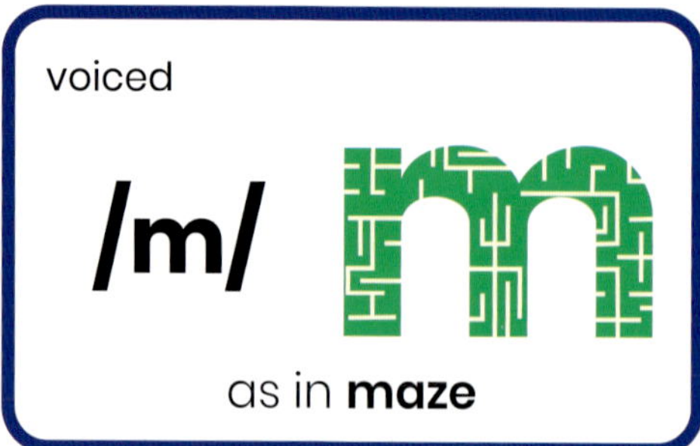

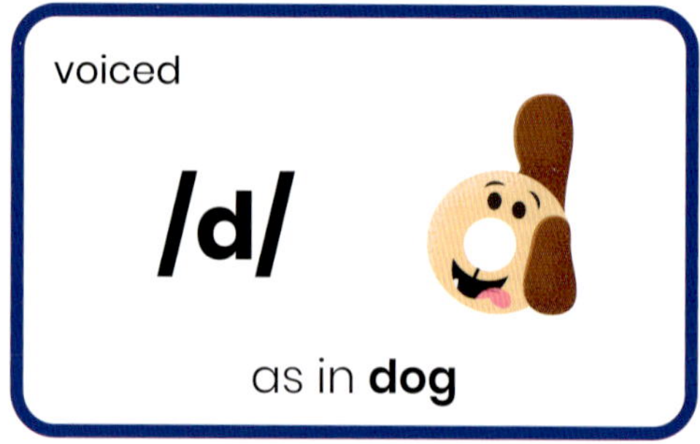

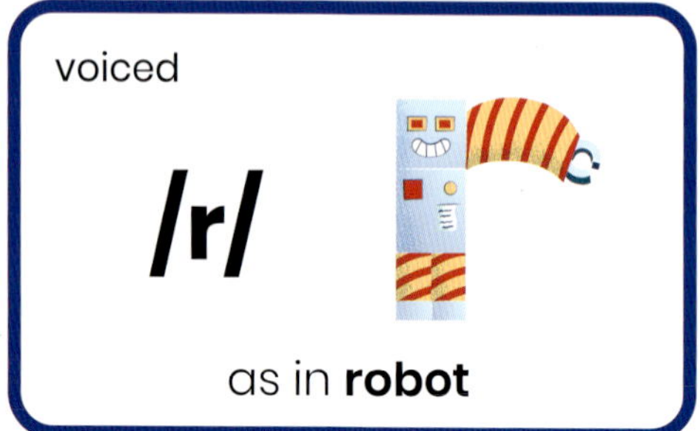

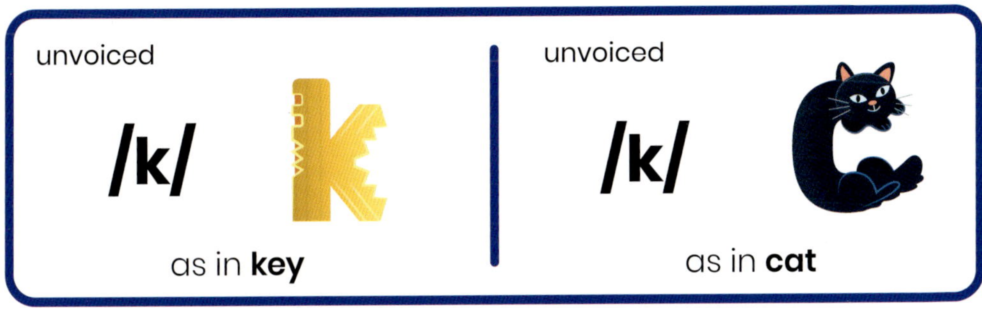
unvoiced
/k/
as in **key**
unvoiced
/k/
as in **cat**

voiced
/b/
as in **ball**

unvoiced
/f/
as in **fox**

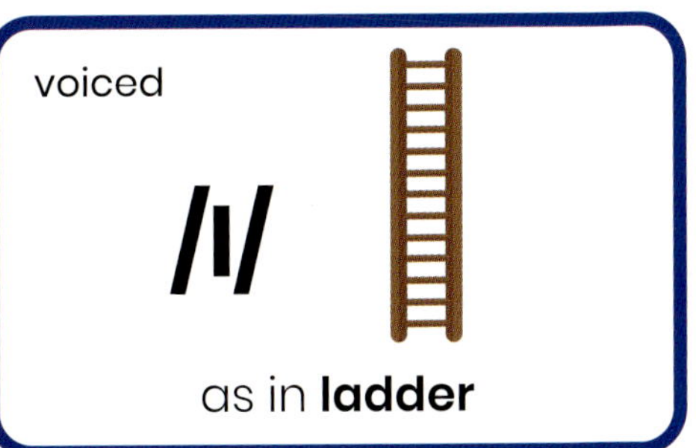
voiced
/l/
as in **ladder**

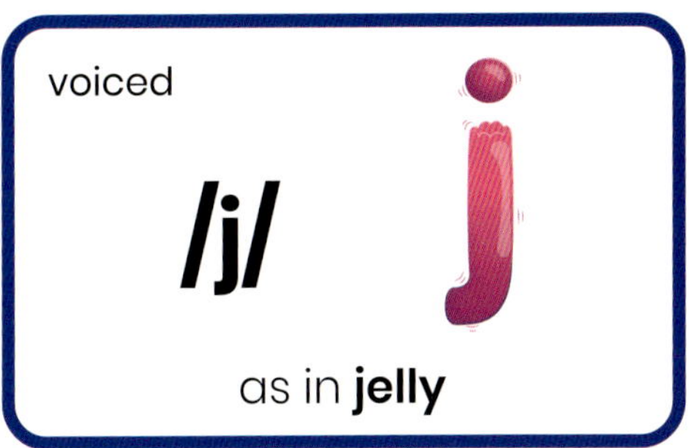
voiced
/j/
as in **jelly**

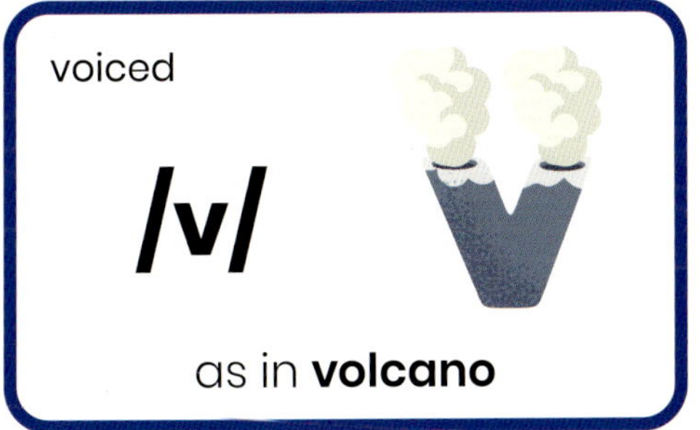
voiced
/v/
as in **volcano**

voiced
/w/
as in **watermelon**

unvoiced
/k/ /s/
as in **wax**

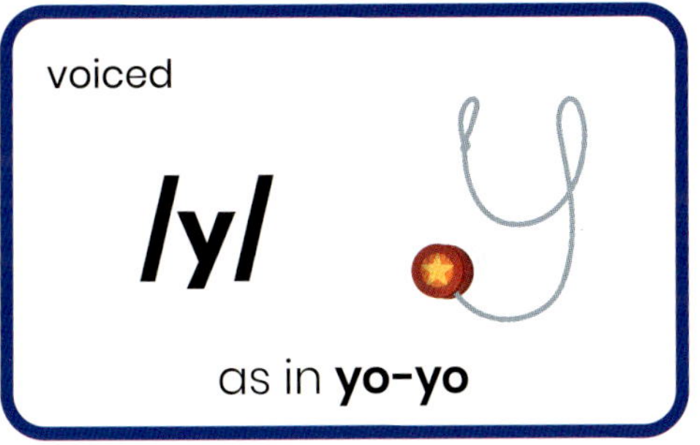
voiced
/y/
as in **yo-yo**

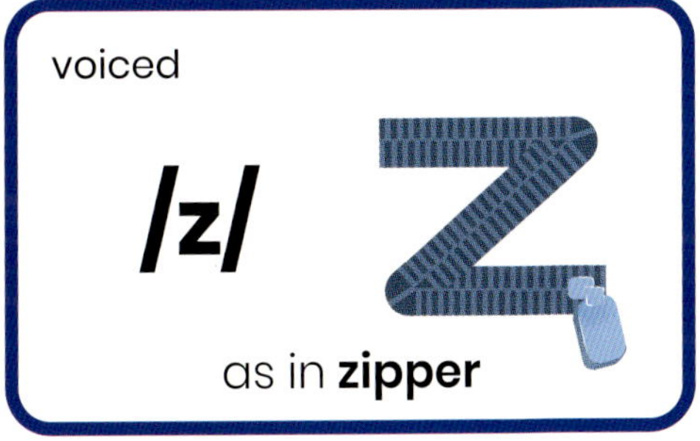
voiced
/z/
as in **zipper**

unvoiced
/k/ /w/
as in **queen**

voiced
/ng/
as in **king**

voiced

/th/ th

as in **weather**

unvoiced

/th/ th

as in **path**

unvoiced

/sh/ sh

as in **sheep**

unvoiced

/ch/ ch

as in **cheese**

voiced

/zh/ s

as in **treasure**

voiced

/a/ a

as in **apple**

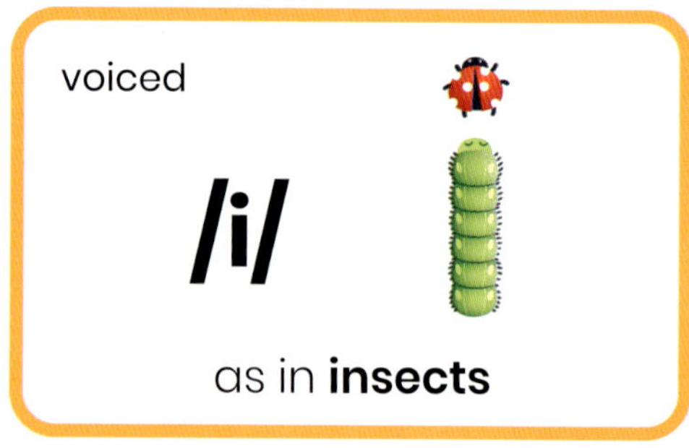

voiced

/i/ i

as in **insects**

voiced

/o/ o

as in **octopus**

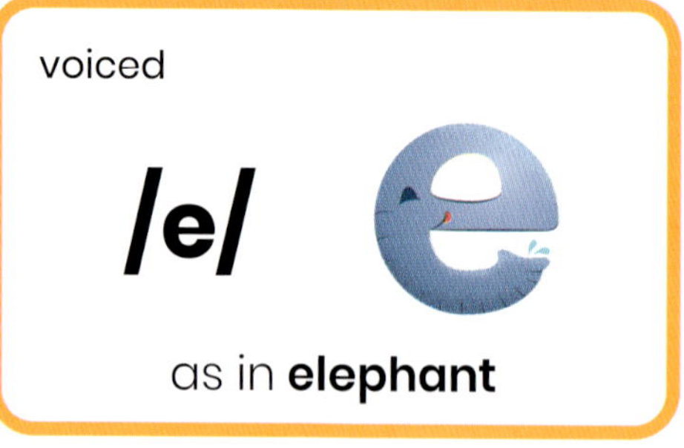

voiced

/e/ e

as in **elephant**

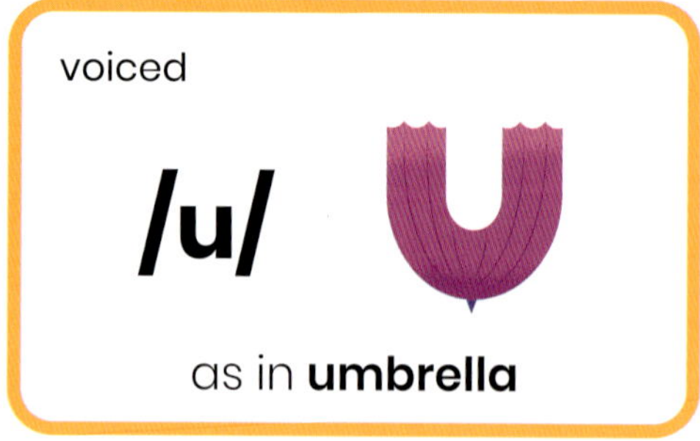

voiced

/u/ u

as in **umbrella**

voiced

/ai/ ai

as in **snail**

voiced

/ee/ ee

as in **bee**

voiced

/igh/ igh

as in **night**

voiced
/oo/
as in **moon**
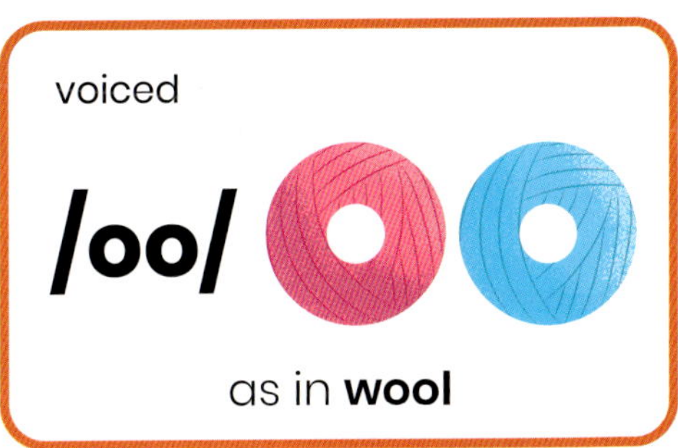
voiced
/oo/
as in **wool**

voiced
/oa/
as in **road**
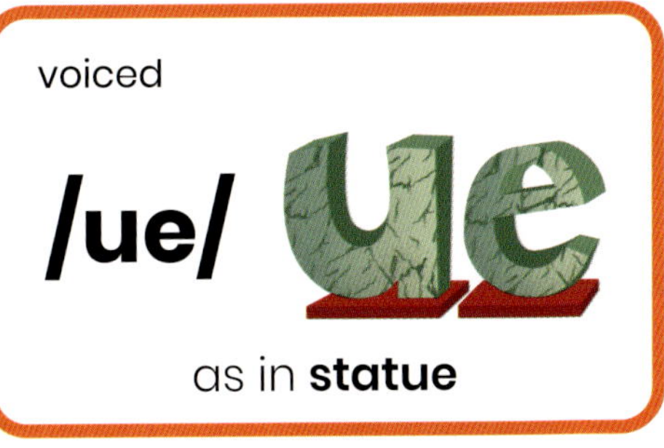
voiced
/ue/
as in **statue**

voiced
/ow/
as in **owl**

voiced
/oy/
as in **toy**

voiced
/ar/
as in **art**

voiced
/aw/
aw
as in **paw**

voiced
/ir/
as in **bird**

voiced
/air/
as in **hair**

voiced
/ear/
as in **gear**

voiced
/ure/
as in **secure**

voiced
schwa ə
as in **banana**

Ss

Say the /s/ sound.

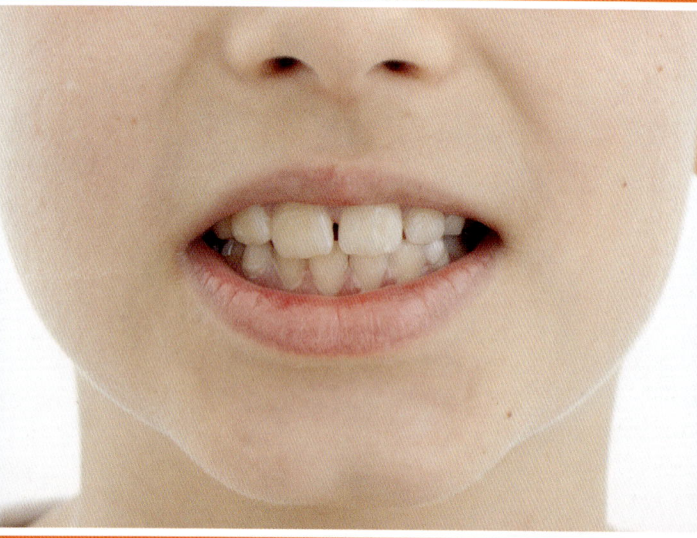

Can you read aloud these words that start with **s**?

sun	**sat**
sit	**sad**

You are a superstar!

What can you see?

Point to and say all the things that start with the /s/ sound in this picture.

sailboat, salad, salt, sand, sandals, sandcastle, sandwich, sausages, scissors, seagull, seal, sky, snail, snake, spider, spoon, starfish, strawberry, stripes, submarine, sun, sunglasses, surfer, surfboard, sword

Look at the picture
Can you find and say the 9 things that start with the /a/ sound in this picture?

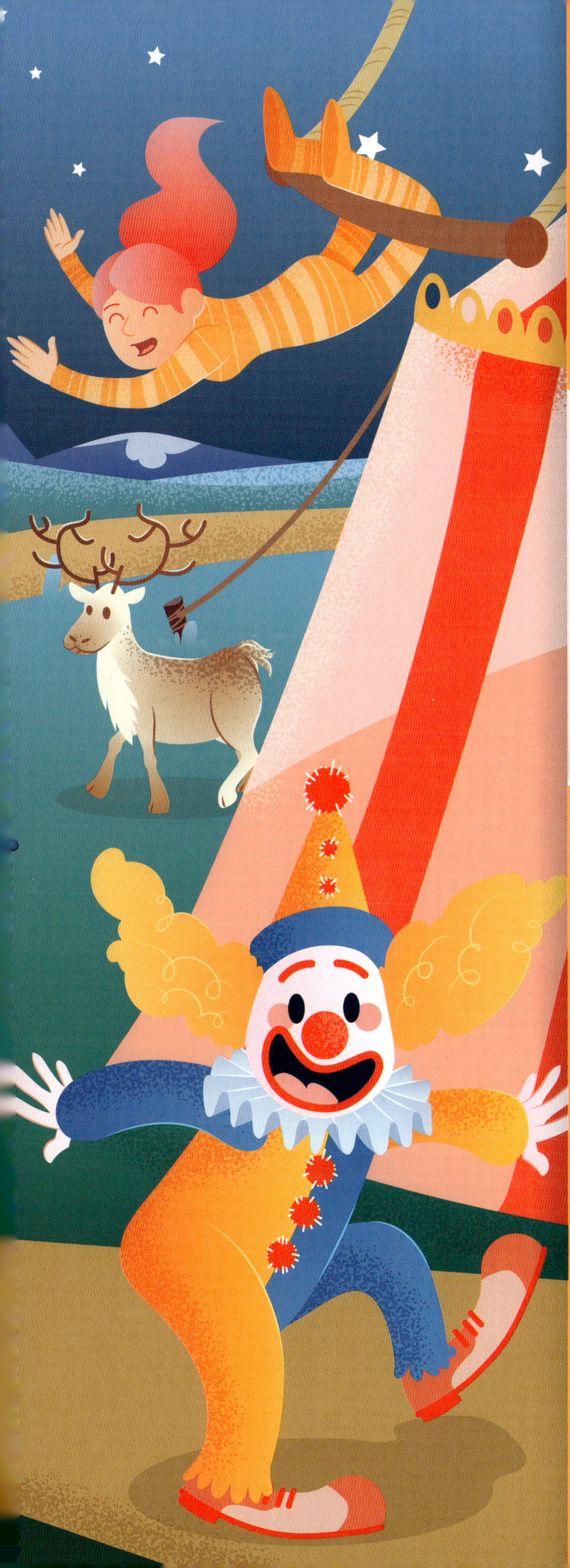

Aa

Say the /a/ sound.

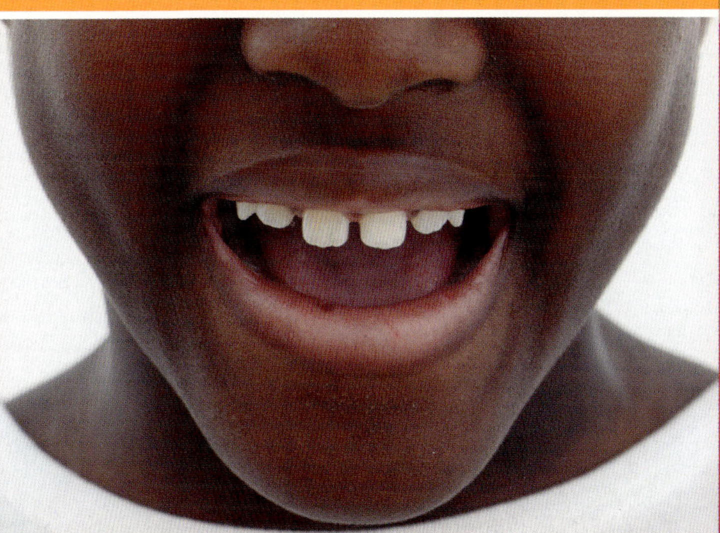

Can you read aloud these words that start with **a**?

at	**add**
ax	**ant**

You are absolutely right!

Tt

Say the /t/ sound.

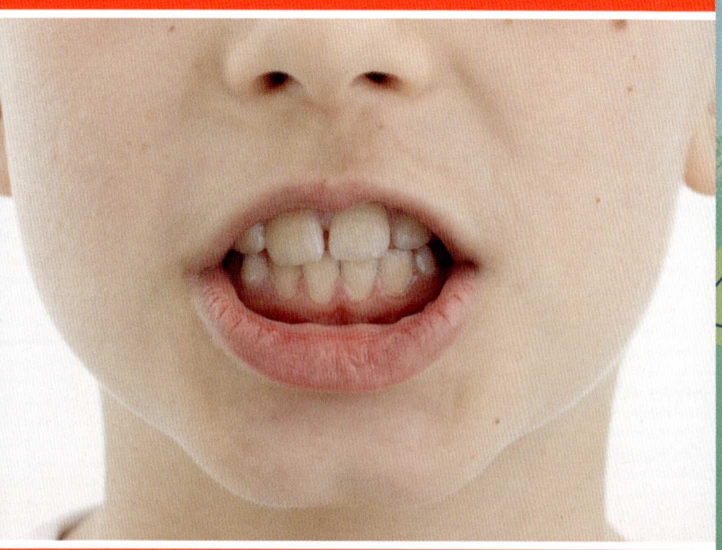

Can you read aloud these words that start with **t**?

tap	**t**ub
top	**t**in

Wow! There's a tiger!

There are 18 other things that start with the /t/ sound in this picture. Can you find them all?

table, tail, tapir, tarantula, tea, teddy bear, tennis, tent, toad, tomatoes, tortoise, tractor, track, train, trampoline, tree, tug-of-war, turtle

Terrific!

Practice your skills!
Can you pick out all of the things in this picture that begin with the /p/ sound?

Pp

Say the /p/ sound.

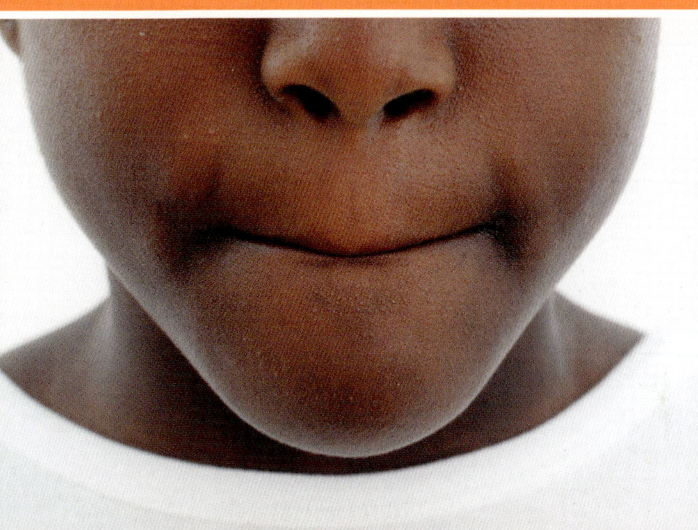

Can you read aloud these words that start with **p**?

pot	**p**en
pan	**p**in

Perfect!

paint, painting, paper, panda, parrot, party, pasta, path, peach, pencil, penguin, piano, picnic, pirate, pizza, plates, playground, polar bear, pony, potatoes, present, pumpkin, puppet, puzzle, python

Ii

Say the /i/ sound.

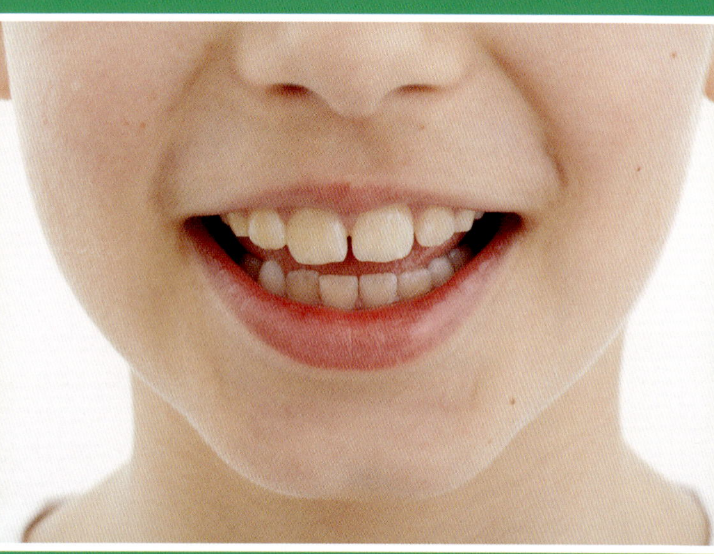

Can you read aloud these words that start with **i**?

ill	**i**n
it	**i**f

Impressive!

That impala is inspirational!

Can you find the 8 other things that start with the /i/ sound in this picture?

igloo, iguana, India, information, injection, insects, instruments, invitation

Have you seen my noodles?

Point to and say the 14 other things in this picture that begin with the /n/ sound.

Nn

Say the /n/ sound.

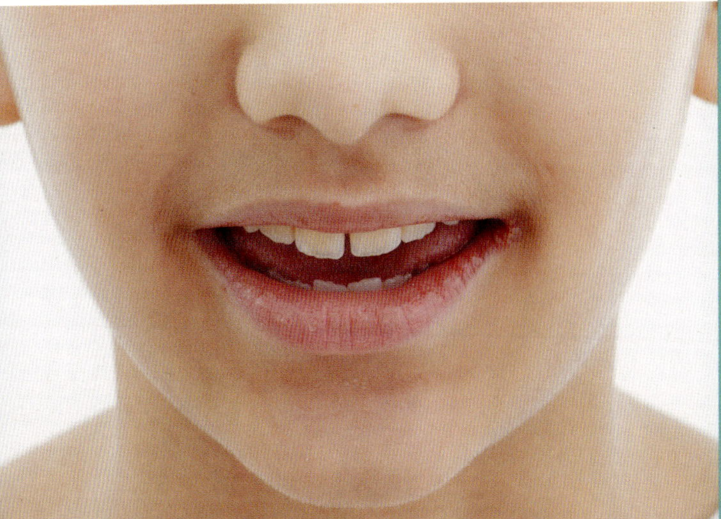

Can you read aloud these words that start with **n**?

net **nap**

not **nut**

Nice work!

nail, narwhal, neck, necklace, nest, net, newspaper, newt, nine, ninja, nose, notebook, nurse, nut

Mm

Say the /m/ sound.

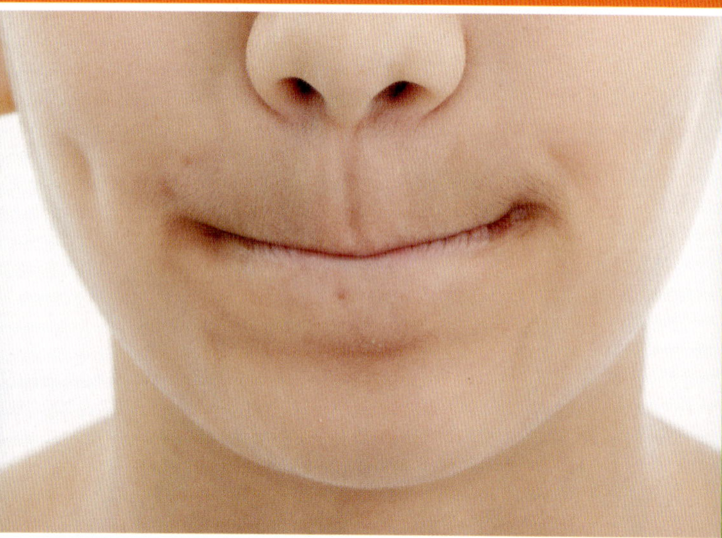

m

Can you read aloud these words that start with **m**?

map	**m**an
mop	**m**ud

You're magic!

I spy a manatee!

There are lots of other things that start with the /m/ sound in this picture. Can you spot them all?

mail, map, man, mat, meerkat, mermaid, milkshake, mole, monkey, monster, moon, mop, moth, motorcycle, mountains, mouse, mud, muffin, mug, mushrooms, music

N
W
E
S

Dd

Say the /d/ sound.

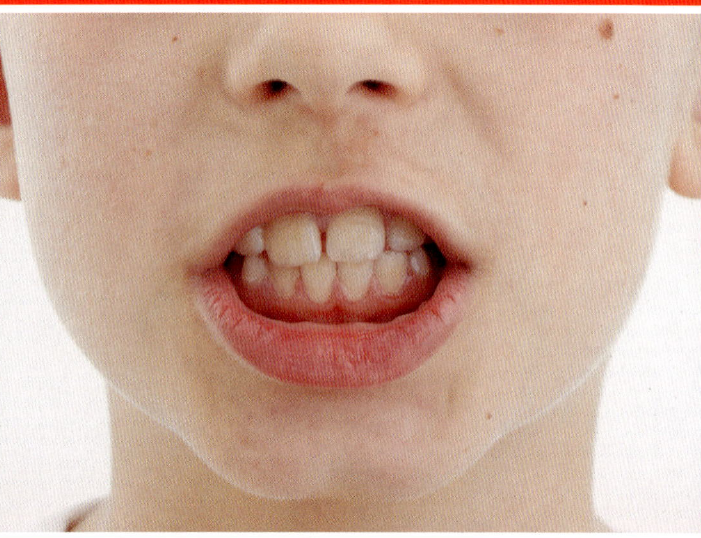

Can you read aloud these words that start with **d**?

dog	**d**id
dig	**d**en

Dazzling work!

Who's driving that digger?

Discover all the other things that start with the /d/ sound in this picture. How many can you see?

There are 20 other things beginning with the /d/ sound: daffodil, daisy, dancer, dandelion, deer, den, diamond, dinosaur, doctor, dog, dolphin, donkey, donut, door, dove, dragonfly, drawbridge, dress, drink, duck

Gg

Say the /g/ sound.

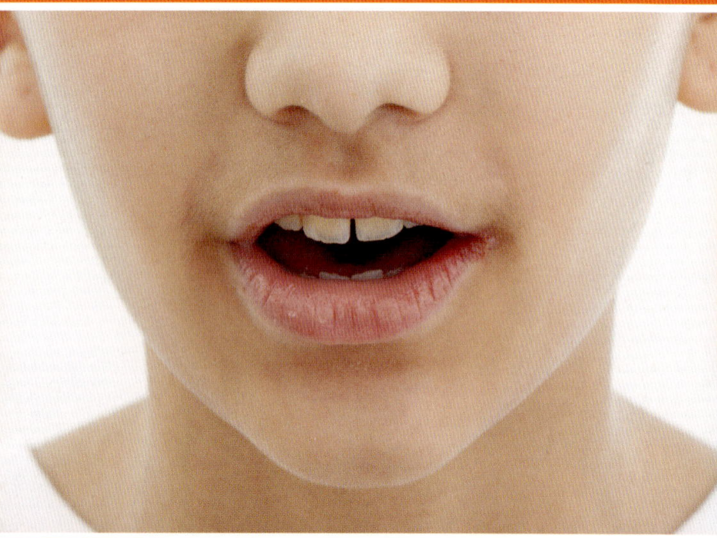

Can you read aloud these words that start with **g**?

gum **g**ap

gut **g**as

Get set, go!

Look for everything that starts with the /g/ sound. Can you find all 18 things?

You're great!

gate, gazelle, gecko, gifts, girl, glass, glasses, goat, gold, golf, goose, gorilla, grapes, grass, grasshopper, guinea pig, guitar, gum

Is that an ostrich with a tray of olives?

See if you can find the 6 other things that start with the /o/ sound in this image.

Oo

Say the /o/ sound.

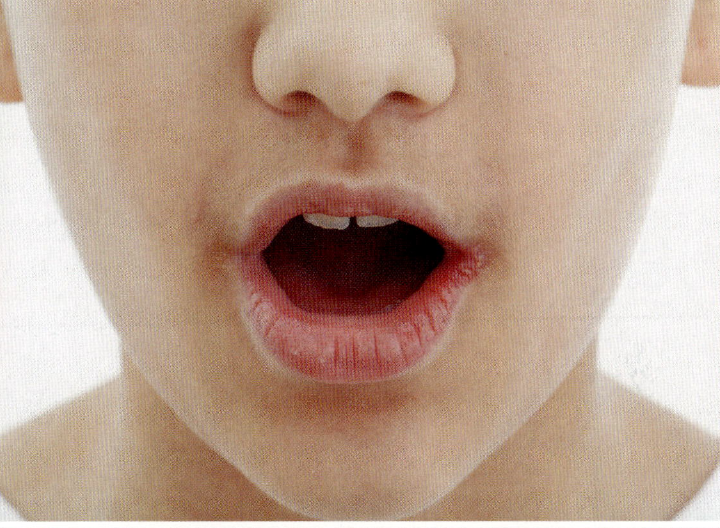

Can you read aloud these words that start with **o**?

on	**o**dd
off	**o**x

How many tentacles does an octopus have?

octagon, octopus, office, omelet, otter, ox

Cc

Say the /k/ sound.

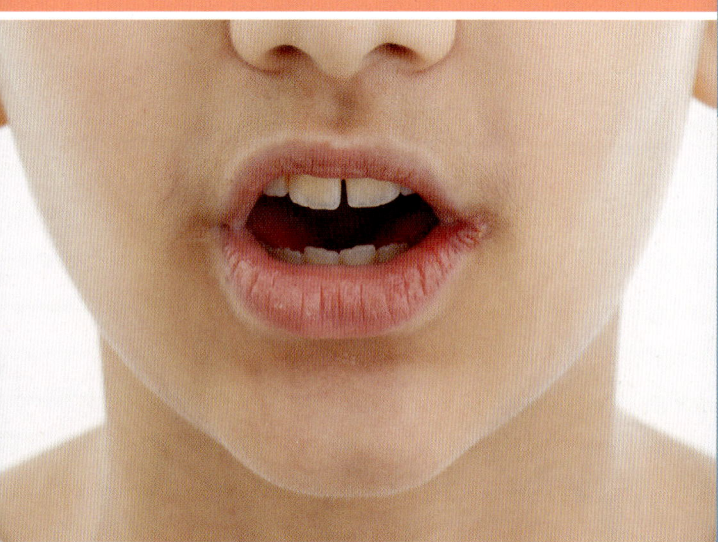

Can you read aloud these words that start with **c**?

can	**c**ab
cot	**c**at

Congratulations! You are doing so well.

Can you spot a crab?

How many other things that start with the /k/ sound can you see in this picture?

There are 25 other things beginning with the /k/ sound: cactus, calendar, camel, candle, cap, car, card, carrot, castle, cat, clock, coat, coconut, coffee, coin, compass, cookie, cooler, cotton candy, cow, crayon, crown, cucumber, cup, cupcake

That's some top karate!

There are lots of other things that start with the /k/ sound in this picture. Can you find all 14 of them?

Kk

Say the /k/ sound.

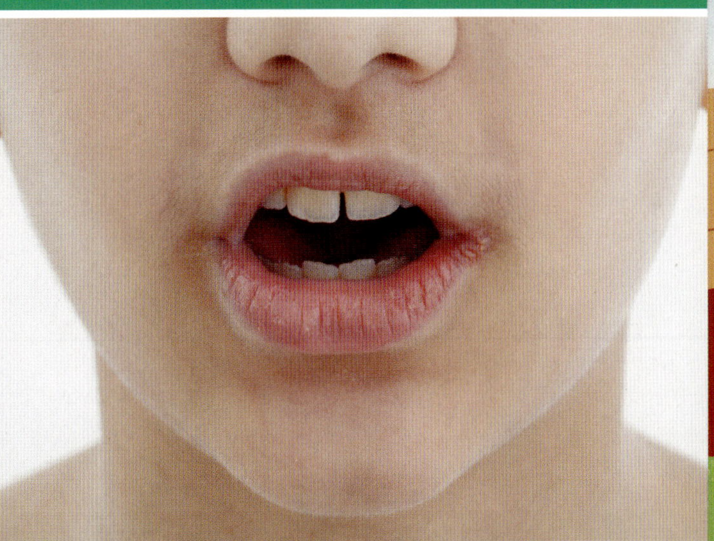

Can you read aloud these words that start with **k**?

kid	**k**it
kin	**K**en

Keep up the great work!
Which of the animals in the picture are known to live in Australia?

Ee

Say the /e/ sound.

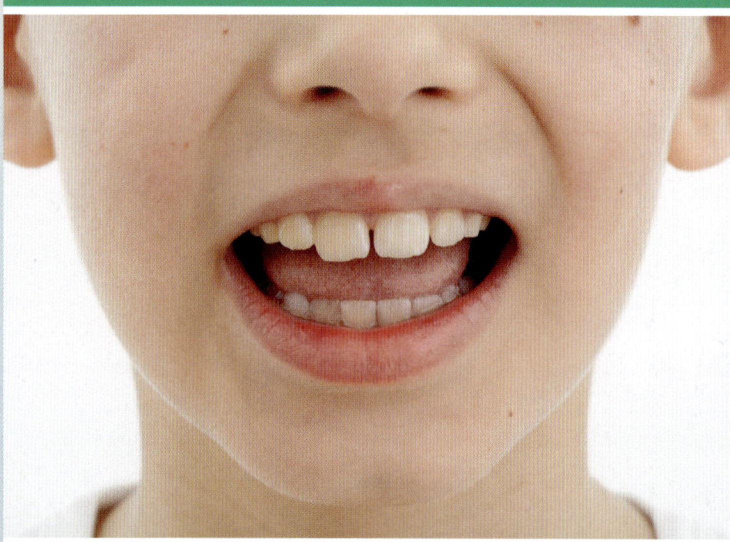

Can you read aloud these words that start with **e**?

end	**elk**
elf	**ebb**

Excellent!

The elves look busy in their workshop!

Do you think you can find the 12 other things that start with the /e/ sound in this picture?

egg, elbow, elephant, elk, empty, engine, engineer, envelope, exercise, exit, experiment, explorer

EXIT

Are you up for a challenge?

Point to and say the 10 things that start with the /u/ sound in the pictures below.

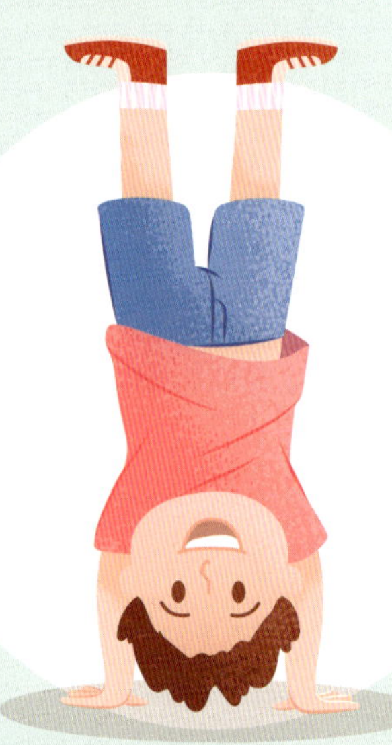

Uu

Say the /u/ sound.

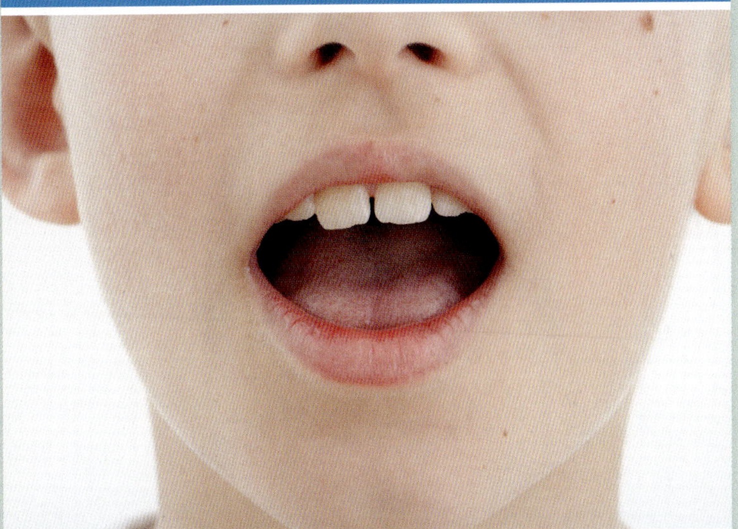

Can you read aloud these words with **u** in them?

up **fun**

us **tub**

Unbelievable!

udder, umbrella, uncle, under, underground, unhappy, unlock, up, upside down, upstairs

Rr

Say the /r/ sound.

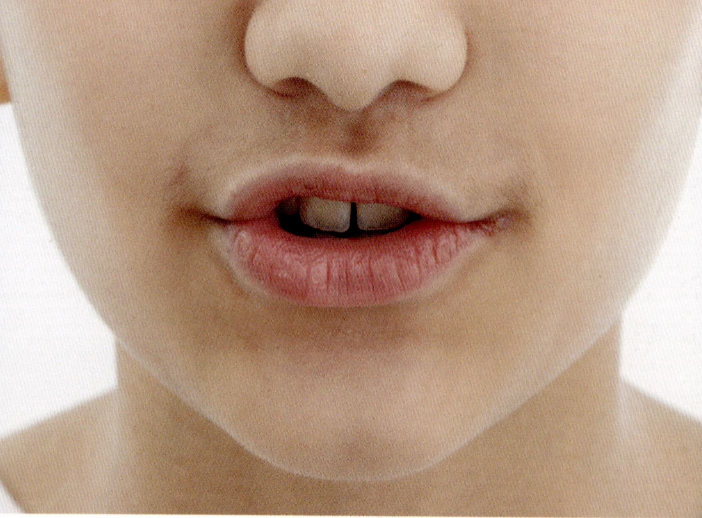

Can you read aloud these words that start with **r**?

red **r**ag

rat **r**od

Really good job!

Look at that beautiful rainbow!

There are 17 other things that start with the /r/ sound in this picture. Do you think you can spot them all?

rabbit, raccoon, radio, rat, rain, raincoat, red, rhinoceros, river, robot, rock, rocket, rod, roller coaster, roller skates, rose, rug

What a pretty hummingbird!

Take a shot at finding all of the other things that start with the /h/ sound in this picture. How many can you spot?

Hh

Say the /h/ sound.

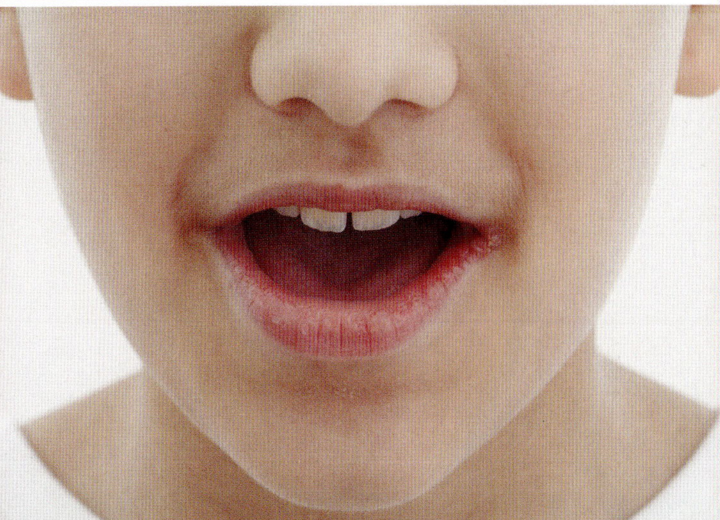

Can you read aloud these words that start with **h**?

hat	**h**op
hip	**h**ad

Hooray! Which of the animals in the picture do you like best?

There are 20 other things beginning with the /h/ sound: hammer, hand, handle, harp, hat, hay, hedgehog, helicopter, helmet, hen, hippopotamus, hive, hockey, honey, hook, horn, horse, hospital, hot-air balloon, house

Bb

Say the /b/ sound.

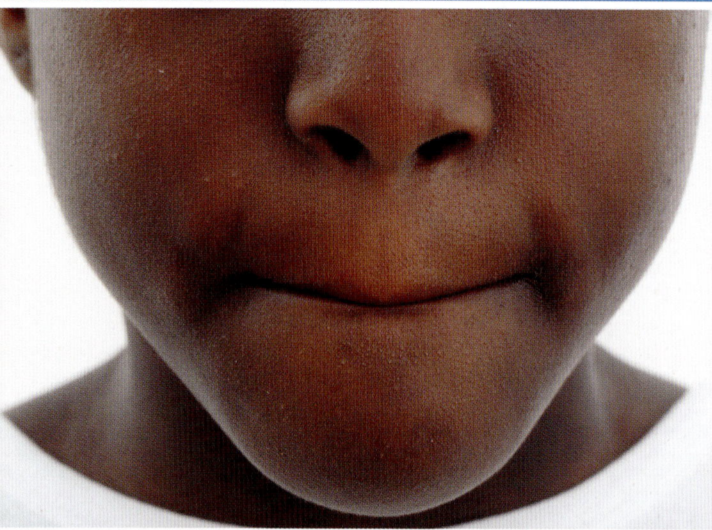

Can you read aloud these words that start with **b**?

bag	**b**at
bed	**b**us

Brilliant!

Begin your search!

How many things that start with the /b/ sound can you see in this picture?

There are 32 things beginning with the /b/ sound: baby, bag, ball, balloon, banana, barn, barrel, bat, beach, bear, beaver, bee, beehive, beetle, bell, belt, bib, bicycle, bird, blueberry, boat, book, boots, bottle, box, boy, bubbles, bulb, burger, bus, butterfly, button

What a funky flamingo!
There are 16 other things that start with the /f/ sound in this picture. Can you find them all?

Say the /f/ sound.

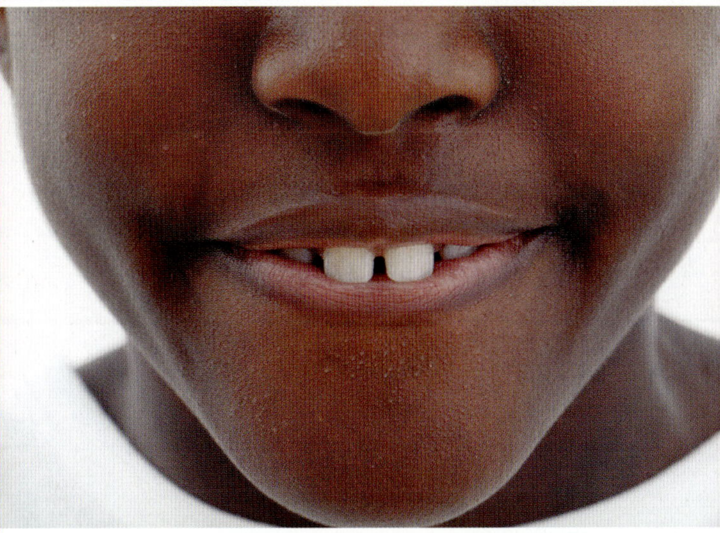

Can you read aloud these words that start with **f**?

fan	**f**un
fit	**f**og

Fantastic work!

family, fan, farmer, field, fire, fish, flags, floor, flowers, flute, fly, fork, fox, frame, frog, fruit

Ll

Say the /l/ sound.

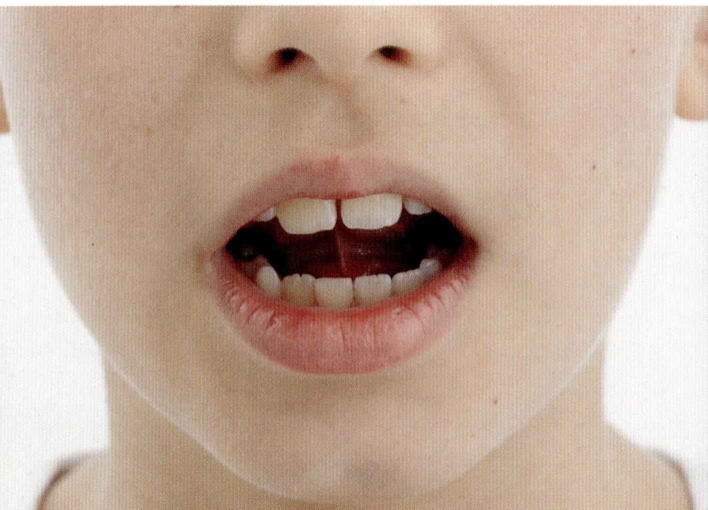

Look at that laid-back lobster!

Can you find the other 16 things that start with the /l/ sound in this picture?

Can you read aloud these words that start with l?

lid	leg
log	lap

Do you like lemons?

ladder, ladybug, lake, lamp, laptop, leaf, legs, lemon, leopard, lettuce, lighthouse, lime, lion, lizard, locust, lollipop

Jj

Say the /j/ sound.

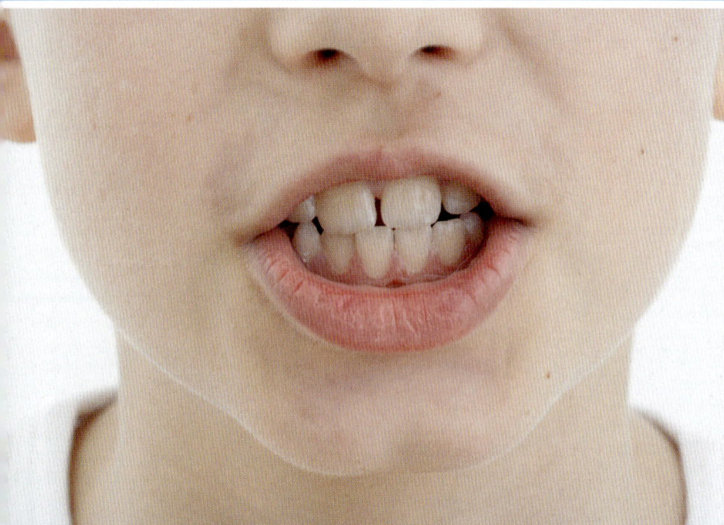

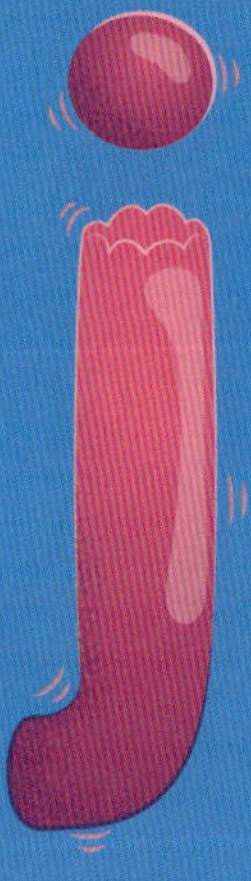

Can you read aloud these words that start with **j**?

jet	**jug**
jam	**jig**

Find and say the 15 things that start with the /j/ sound in this picture.

jacket, jaguar, jam, jar, jeans, Jell-O, jellyfish, jet, jewels, jigsaw puzzle, judge, juggle, juice, jungle, jury

Great job!

Find and say the 10 things that start with the /v/ sound in this picture.

vacuum cleaner, van, vase, vegetables, veil, vet, village, violin, volcano, volleyball

Vv

Say the /v/ sound.

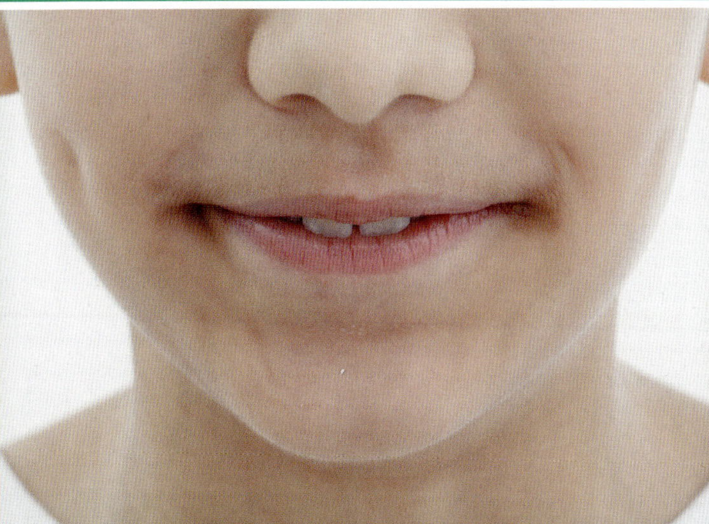

Can you read aloud these words that start with **v**?

vet	**v**est
van	**v**ent

Very good!

Ww

Say the /w/ sound.

Can you read aloud these words that start with **w**?

web	**wig**
wet	**win**

Wow, you are doing so well! Do you like it when the weather is sunny, rainy, or snowy?

Find and say the 14 things that start with the /w/ sound in this picture.

walrus, washing machine, wasp, watch, water, waterfall, watermelon, web, well, windmill, wolf, wood, woodpecker, worm

Point to and say the things that end with the /k/ and /s/ sounds blended together on this page. In these words, these sounds are spelled **x**.

The sounds /k/ and /s/ together are spelled **x**. Blend the /k/ and /s/ sounds together to try saying this.

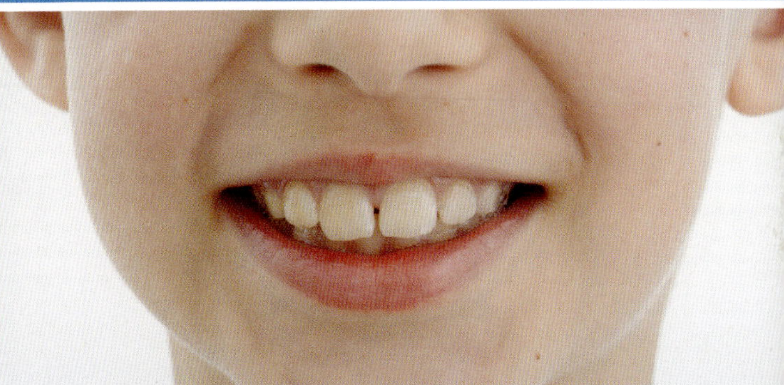

Can you read aloud these words that end with **x**?

bo**x**	fi**x**
wa**x**	mi**x**

box, fox, mix, ox, six, wax

Relax! You are doing great!

Yy

Say the /y/ sound.

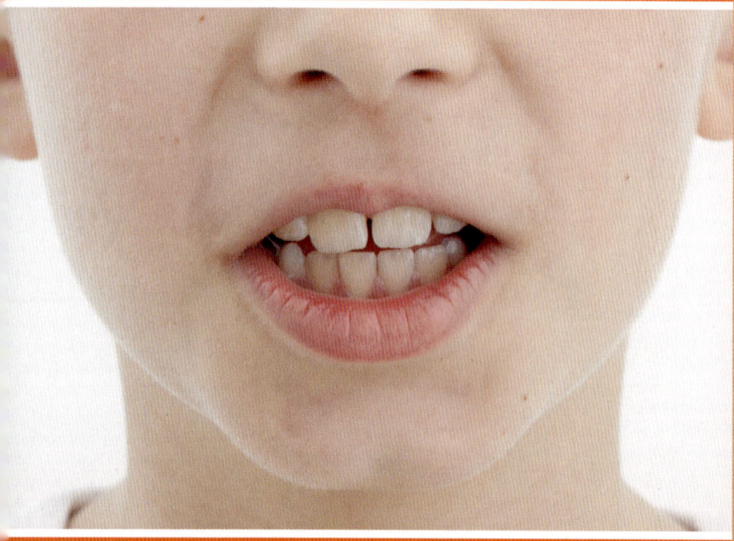

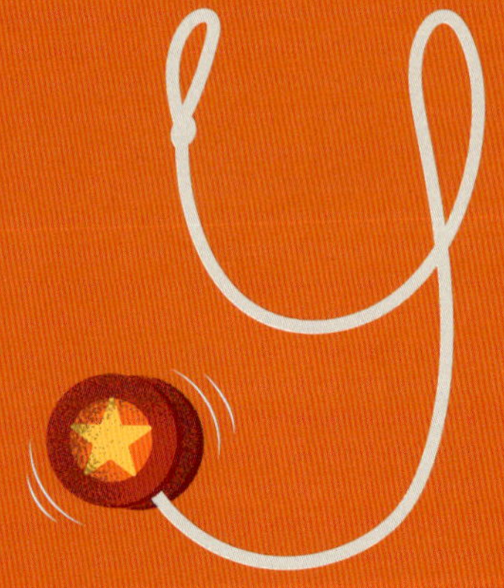

Can you read aloud these words that start with **y**?

yam **y**es

yak **y**um

Point to and say the things that start with the /y/ sound on this page.

yacht, yak, yarn, yoga, yogurt, yo-yo

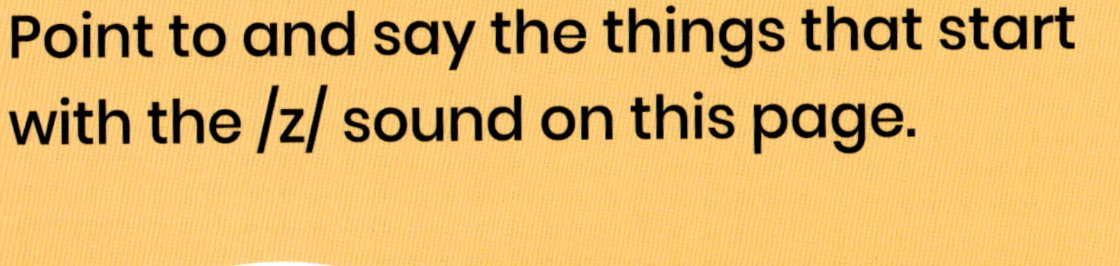

Point to and say the things that start with the /z/ sound on this page.

zap, zebra, zero, zest, zigzag, zoo

Zz

Say the /z/ sound.

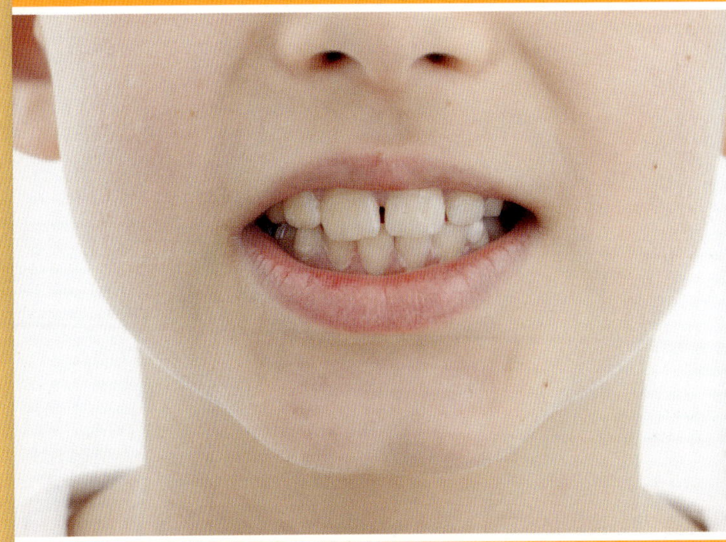

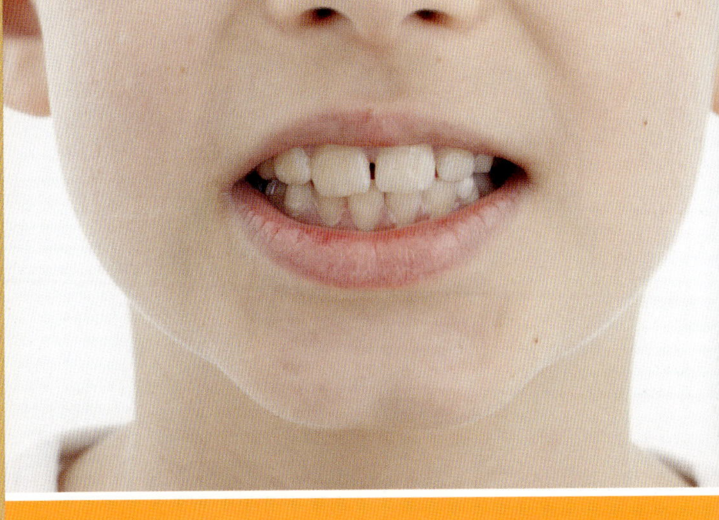

Can you read aloud these words that start with **z**?

zip	**zest**
zap	**zigzag**

Amazing!

CVC

Words made up of consonant, vowel, consonant sounds.

short vowel a

Say the sound.

There are many words made up of three sounds that have the /a/ sound as the second sound.

Can you read aloud these **CVC** words with **a** in them?

bat	rat
cap	ram

Do you like jam?

bat, can, cap, cat, fan, hat, jam, man, map, pan, rat, sad, van

Watch out for that ram!

Point to and say the 13 other CVC things in this picture that have the /a/ sound as the second sound.

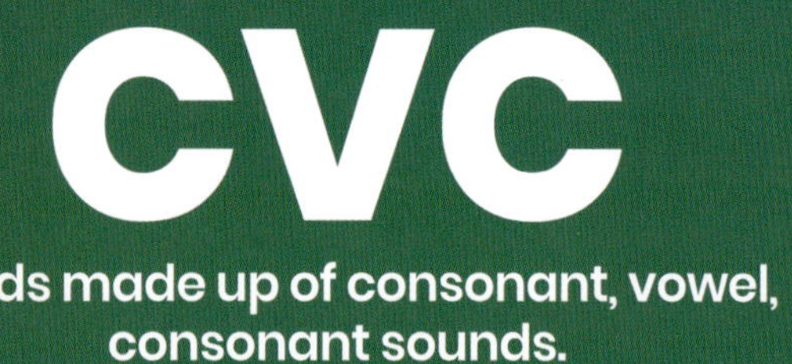

Words made up of consonant, vowel, consonant sounds.

short vowel e

Say the sound.

There are many words made up of three sounds that have the /e/ sound as the second sound.

Can you read aloud these **CVC** words with **e** in them?

leg	bed
get	yes

Do you have a pet?

bed, bell, hen, jet, peg, pen, pet, red, ten, vet, web

It's so wet!

Point to and say the 11 other CVC things in this picture that have the /e/ sound as the second sound.

That fig looks yummy!

Point to and say the 10 other CVC things in this picture that have the /i/ sound as the second sound.

CVC

Words made up of consonant, vowel, consonant sounds.

short vowel i

Say the sound.

There are many words made up of three sounds that have the /i/ sound as the second sound.

Can you read aloud these **CVC** words with **i** in them?

dig	tip
sip	bit

That's a big achievement!

dig, fin, kid, lid, mix, sip, sit, six, tip, wig

What's cooking in the pot?

Point to and say the 11 other CVC things in this picture that have the /o/ sound as the second sound.

CVC

Words made up of consonant, vowel, consonant sounds.

short vowel o

Say the sound.

There are many words made up of three sounds that have the /o/ sound as the second sound.

Can you read aloud these **CVC** words with **o** in them?

job	top
pop	cog

Can you hop like a bunny rabbit?

box, dog, doll, dot, fox, hot, jog, log, pod, rod, sob

Run for the bus!

Point to and say the 13 other CVC things in this picture that have the /u/ sound as the second sound.

CVC

Words made up of consonant, vowel, consonant sounds.

short vowel u

Say the sound.

There are many words made up of three sounds that have the /u/ sound as the second sound.

Can you read aloud these **CVC** words with **u** in them?

yum	cut
bud	tub

Who do you like to hug?

bug, bun, cup, hug, mud, mug, nut, pug,
pup, rug, sum, sun, tub

ff

The /f/ sound can also be spelled **ff**.

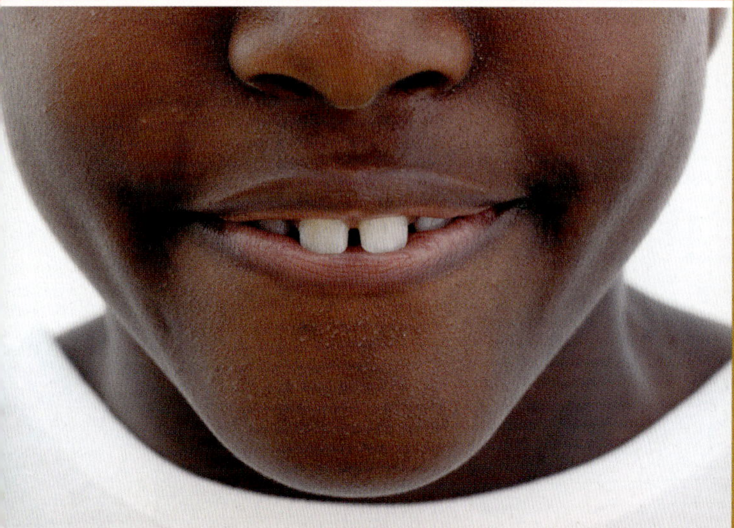

Find and say the 10 things in this picture that have the /f/ sound in them. In these words, the /f/ sound is spelled **ff**.

Can you read aloud these words that end with **ff**?

fluff	**cuff**
puff	**ruff**

What type of muffin do you like the best?

cliff, coffee, cuff, earmuffs, handcuff,
muffin, puff, ruff, sheriff, waffles

Find and say the 12 things in this picture that have the /s/ sound in them. In these words, the /s/ sound is spelled **ss**.

ss

The /s/ sound can also be spelled **ss**.

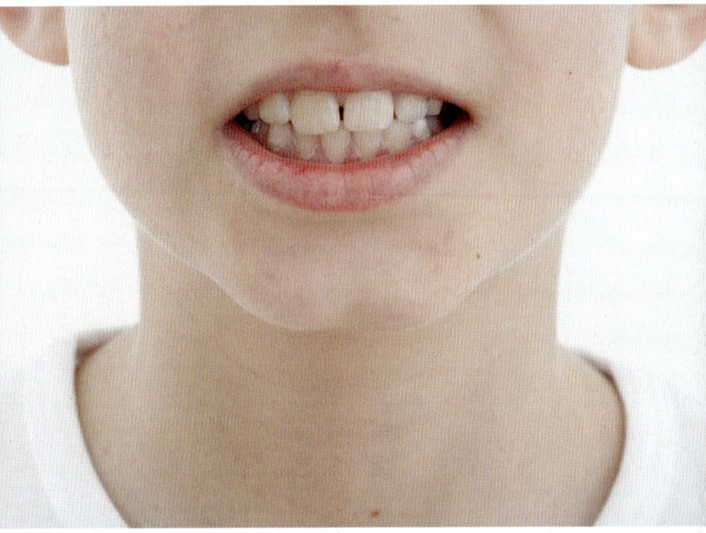

Can you read aloud these words that end with **ss**?

miss	fuss
less	boss

What animal goes "hiss"?

address, blossom, chess, cross, dress, glass, glasses, grass, hiss, miss, princess, toss

zz

The /z/ sound can also be spelled **zz**.

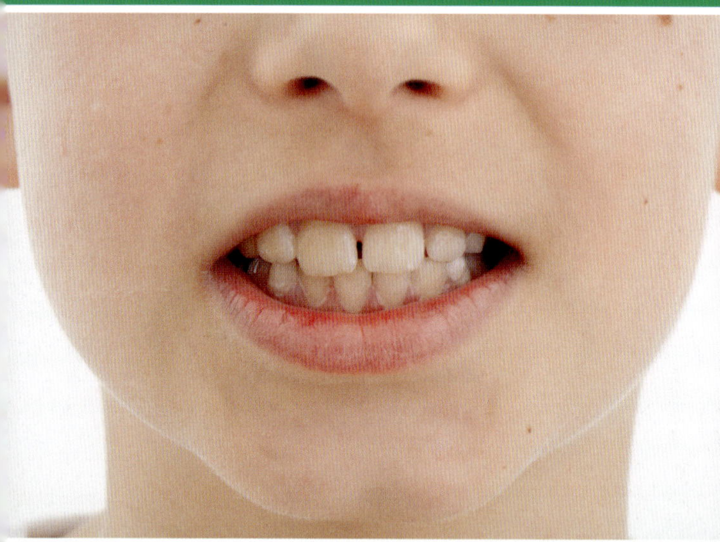

Can you read aloud these words that end with **zz**?

buzz **fizz**

fuzz **jazz**

Do you enjoy doing a puzzle?

Find and say the 7 things in this picture that have the /z/ sound in them. In these words, the /z/ sound is spelled **zz**.

buzz, dizzy, fizzy, frizzy, Jacuzzi, jazz, puzzle

Find and say the 11 things in the picture that have the /l/ sound in them. In these words, the /l/ sound is spelled **ll**.

ll

The /l/ sound can also be spelled **ll**.

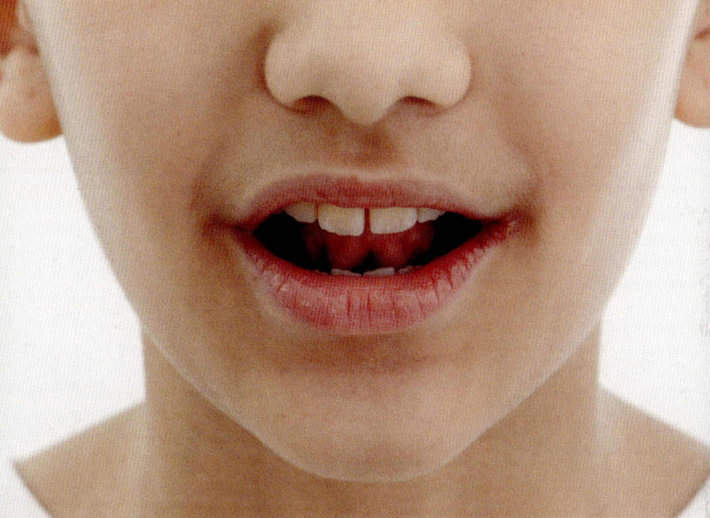

Can you read aloud these words that end with **ll**?

tell	**doll**
gull	**hill**

Well done!

ball, bell, bull, doll, gull, hill, mill, troll, wall, waterfall, well

ck

The /k/ sound can also be spelled **ck**.

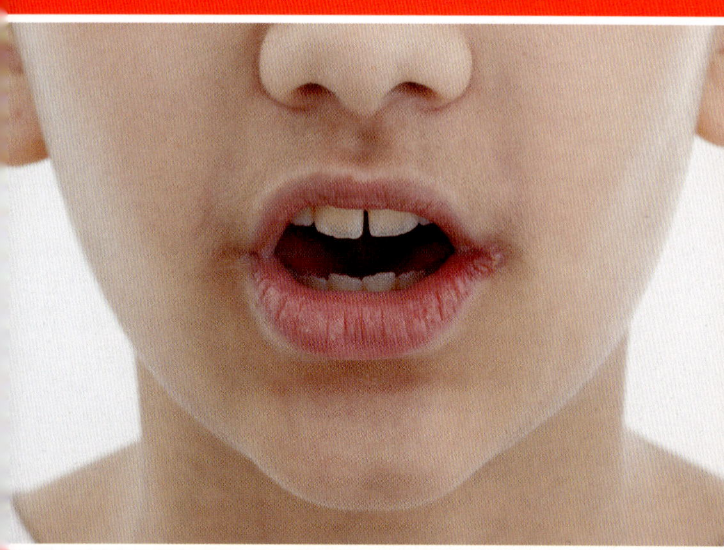

Can you read aloud these words that end with **ck**?

du**ck**	ne**ck**
lo**ck**	sa**ck**

That was super slick!

Find and say the 13 things in the picture that have the /k/ sound in them. In these words, the /k/ sound is spelled **ck**.

backpack, brick, clock, dock, duck, lock, muck, rock, shipwreck, sick, sock, stick, stuck

Find and say the 9 things in the picture that end with the /ng/ sound.

ng

Say the /ng/ sound.

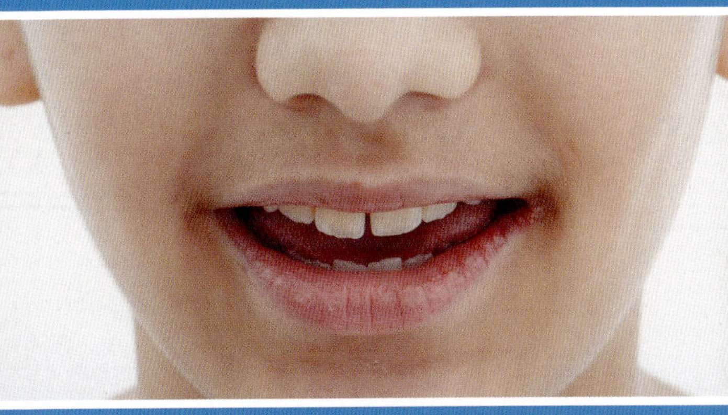

Can you read aloud these words that end with **ng**?

ring	sing
long	king

cling, fang, hang, king, ring, sing, string, strong, swing

Now you're getting in the swing of it!

CVCC

Words made up of consonant, vowel, consonant, consonant sounds.

Many words are made up of four sounds blended together. In some of these words, a consonant and a vowel are followed by two consonants side by side.

Now read these words. Sound out each sound and blend it together like this “g-o-l-f... golf!”

lift	golf
lamp	help

Your best work yet!

What a big gust of wind!

Point to and say aloud the other 12 CVCC words in this scene.

camp, desk, gift, golf, hand, lamp, milk, nest, pond, tent, west, sand

Is that a crab playing the drum?

Point to and say aloud the 12 other CCVC words in this scene.

CCVC

Words made up of consonant, consonant, vowel, consonant sounds.

Many words are made up of four sounds blended together. In some of these words, there are two consonants side by side followed by a vowel and a consonant.

Now read these words. Sound out each sound and blend it together like this "c-l-a-p... clap!"

clog	**slip**
clap	**frog**

Give yourself a clap!

clam, clap, dress, frog, plum, skip, slip, slug, stop, swim, twig, twin

CCVCC

Words made up of consonant, consonant, vowel, consonant, consonant sounds.

Many words are made up of five sounds blended together. In some of these words, there are two consonants side by side before and after the vowel.

Now read these words. Sound out each sound and blend it together like this "t-w-i-s-t... twist!"

print	crust
blast	twist

What animal has a trunk?

blond, crust, drops, plank, skunk, spots, stamp, stand, stink, stump, trunk, twins, twist

Spend wisely at the market!

Point to and say aloud the other 13 CCVCC words in this scene.

-ed /d/

When talking about something done in the past, **ed** is often added to the end of the word. Sometimes, **ed** spells the /d/ sound.

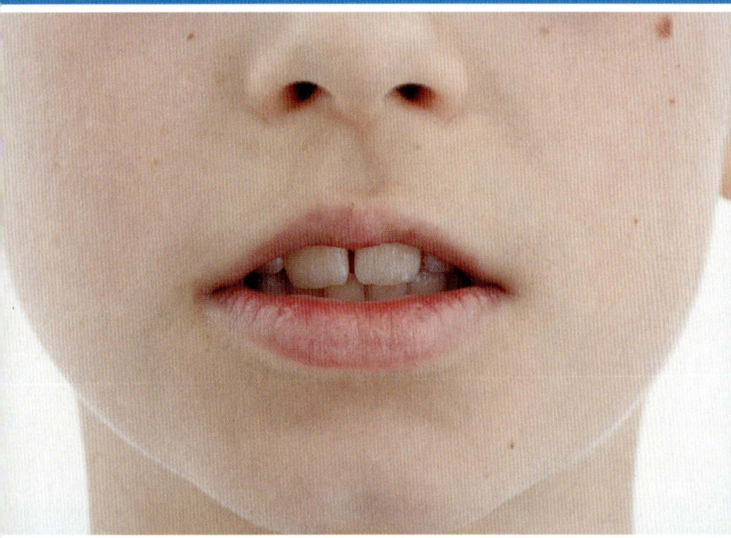

Can you read aloud these words that end with **ed**?

filled **pulled**

robbed **banged**

Point to and say the actions on this page that end in the /d/ sound. In these words, the /d/ sound is spelled **ed**.

called, cleared, drummed, filled, pulled, rained

Yay! You pulled it off!

Find and say the 7 actions on this page that end in the /t/ sound. In these words, the /t/ sound is spelled **ed**.

chopped, fished, hopped, skipped, splashed, washed, watched

-ed /t/

When talking about something done in the past, **ed** is often added to the end of the word. Sometimes, **ed** spells the /t/ sound.

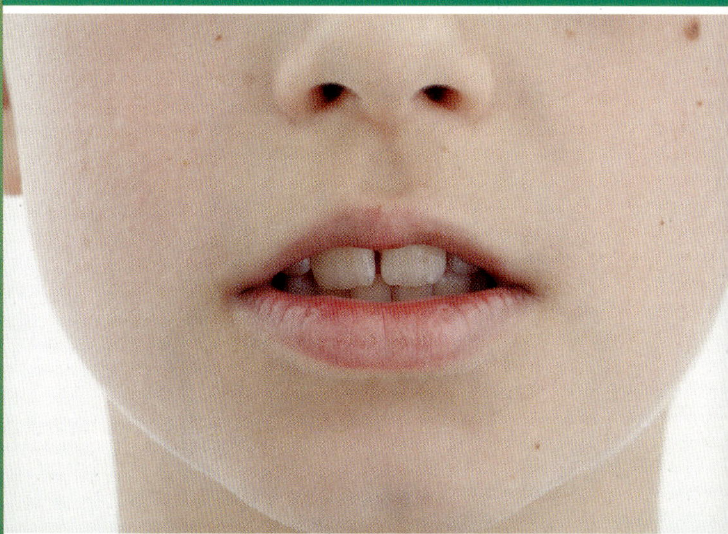

Can you read aloud these words that end with **ed**?

skipp**ed** wash**ed**

hopp**ed** miss**ed**

-ed /id/

When talking about something done in the past, **ed** is often added to the end of the word. If the base word ends with a **t** or a **d**, **ed** spells the /i/ and /d/ sounds blended together.

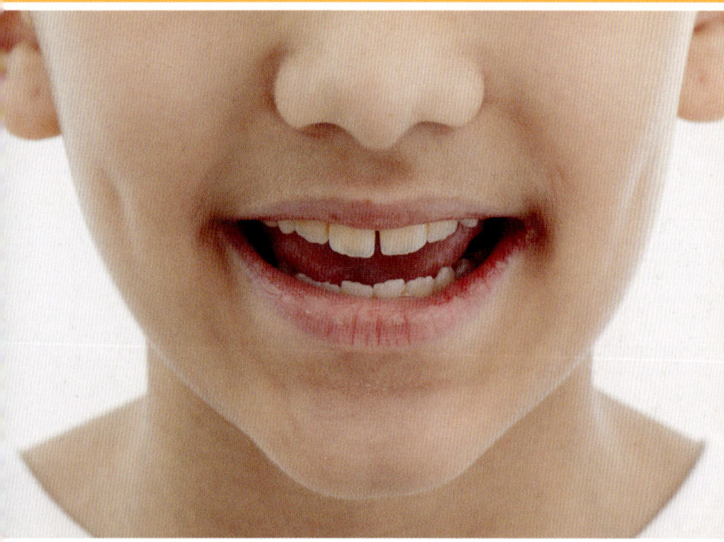

Can you read aloud these words that end with **ed**?

print**ed** lift**ed**
end**ed** patt**ed**

Have you painted a picture recently?

Point to and say the actions on this page. In these words, the /i/ and /d/ sounds are blended together and spelled **ed**.

lifted, melted, patted, planted, printed, skidded

Find and say the 10 actions on this page that end with the /ee/ and /ng/ sounds blended together.

catching, clapping, dancing, kicking, ringing, singing, sinking, sitting, swimming, throwing

-ing

Many words end in **ing**. Blend the /ee/ and /ng/ sounds together to try saying this.

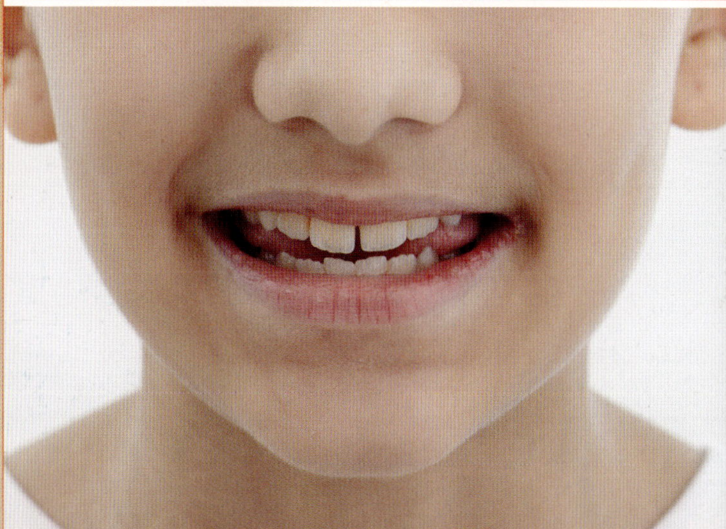

Can you read aloud these words that end in **ing**?

sink**ing** snipp**ing**

hand**ing** clapp**ing**

th (voiced)

The spelling **th** has two different sounds. Say the voiced /th/ sound in the word **mother**.

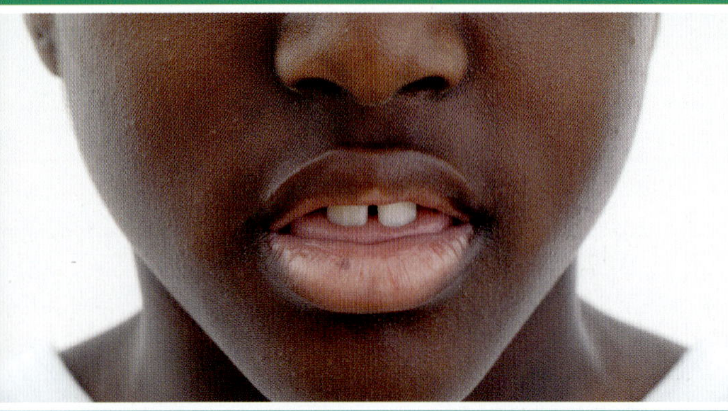

Can you read aloud these words that have this /th/ sound in them?

this	**th**en
that	**th**em

Point to and say the things that have the voiced /th/ sound in them on this page.

brother, feather, mother, that, this, weather

For information on voiced and unvoiced sounds, *see page 143.*

That's superb!

Find and say the 10 things that have the unvoiced /th/ sound in them on this page.

bathroom, earth, moth, mouth, path, teeth, thick, thin, thistle, thumb

th (unvoiced)

The spelling **th** has two sounds. Say the unvoiced /th/ sound in the word **teeth**.

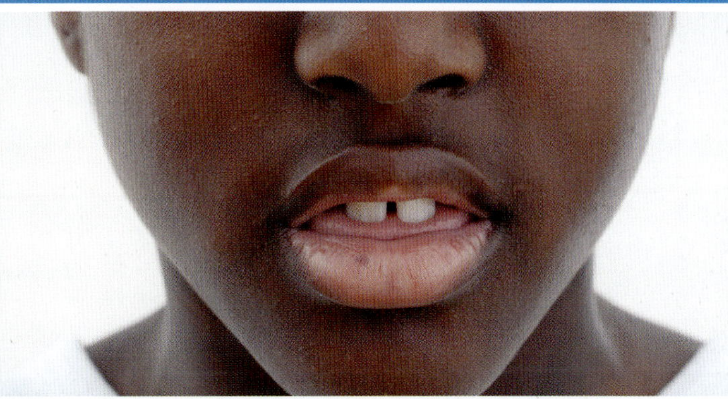

Can you read aloud these words that have this /th/ sound in them?

mo**th**	**th**in
pa**th**	tee**th**

sh

Say the /sh/ sound.

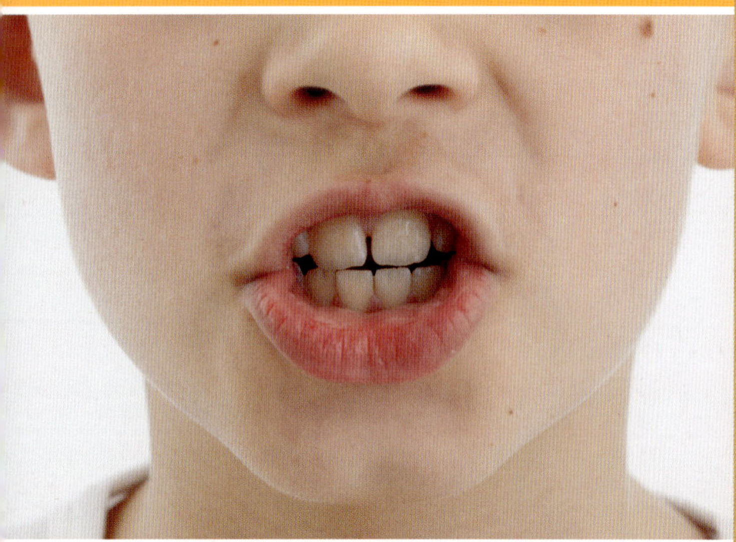

Can you read aloud these words that start or end with **sh**?

shut	**shrub**
gush	**dish**

Well done, you did that in a flash!

Point to and say the things on this page that start or end with the /sh/ sound.

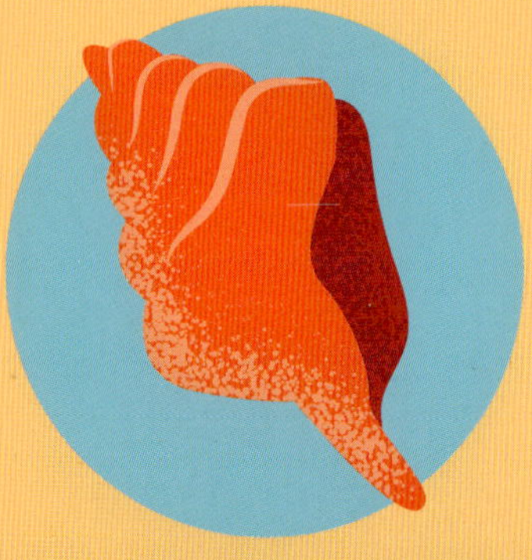

brush, fish, shark, sheep, shell, shirt

Find and say the 12 things that have the /ch/ sound in them on this page.

bench, branch, chain, champ, cheek, cheerleader, cheese, chess, chick, chimp, chocolate, lunch

Say the /ch/ sound.

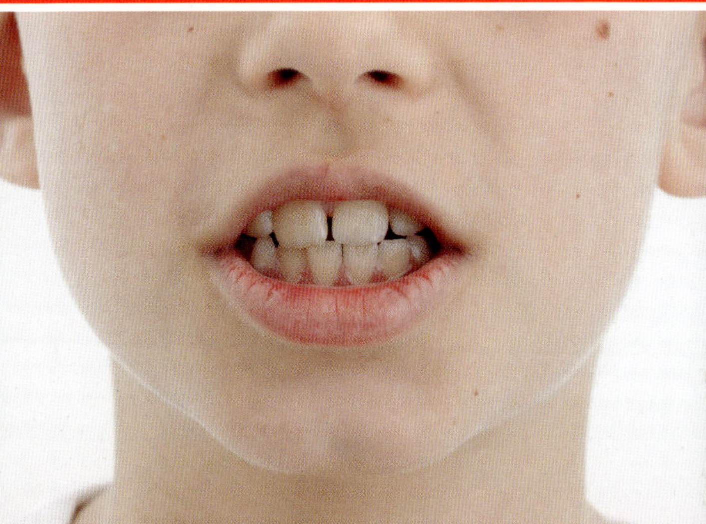

Can you read aloud these words that start or end with **ch**?

check	in**ch**
chill	lun**ch**

You're a champ!

tch

The /ch/ sound can also be spelled **tch**. When a word has a short vowel followed by the /ch/ sound, it is usually spelled **tch**.

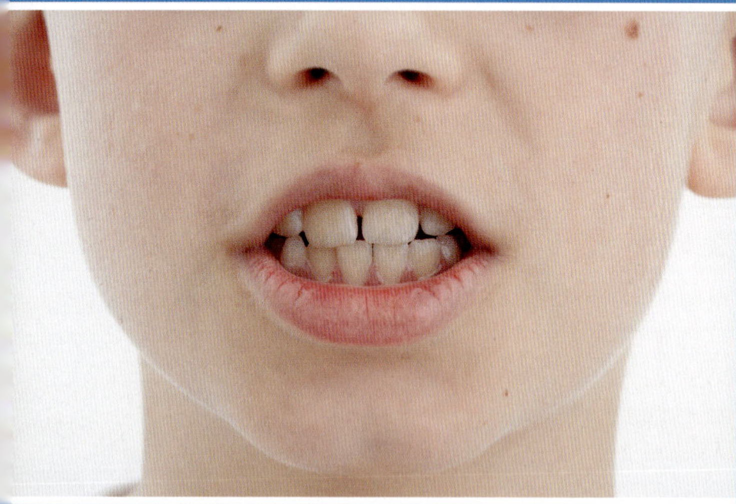

Can you read aloud these words that end with **tch**?

clu**tch**	stre**tch**
ma**tch**	swi**tch**

What animal is in the hutch?

Point to and say the things on this page that have the /ch/ sound in them. In these words, the /ch/ sound is spelled **tch**.

fetch, hutch, kitchen, match, switch, watch

Point to and say the things on this page that end with the /v/ sound. In these words, the /v/ sound is spelled **ve**.

ve

The sound /v/ can also be spelled **ve**. Words in English cannot end with a **v**, so if a word ends with the /v/ sound, it is spelled **ve**.

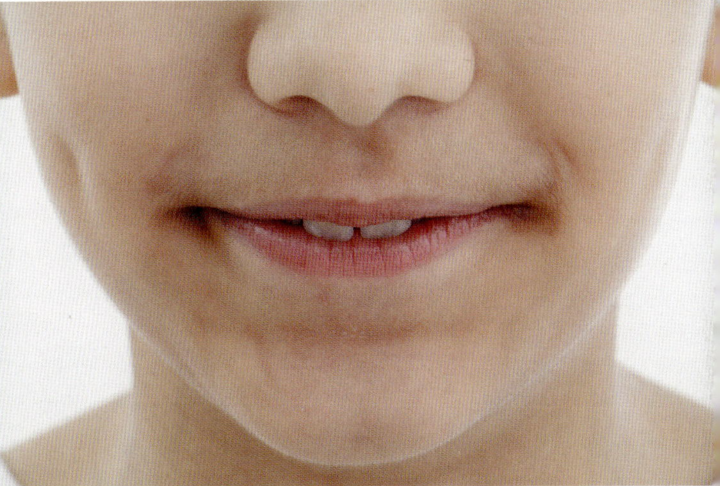

Can you read aloud these words that end with **ve**?

give	have
live	olive

Do you like olives?

give, olive, solve, valve

wh

The /w/ sound can be spelled **wh**.

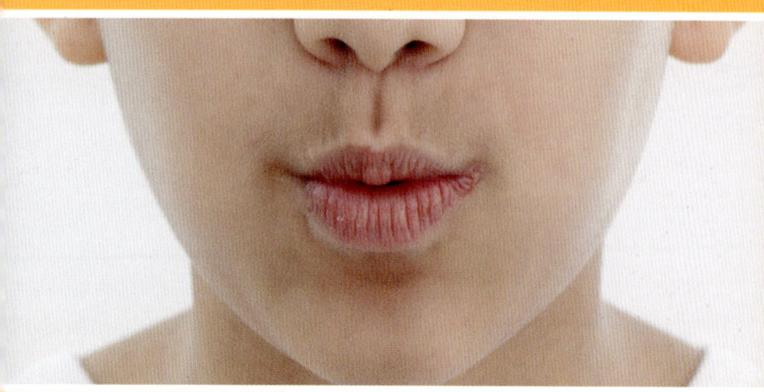

Can you read aloud these words that start with **wh**?

whiff **whip**

whizz **whisk**

Can you whistle?

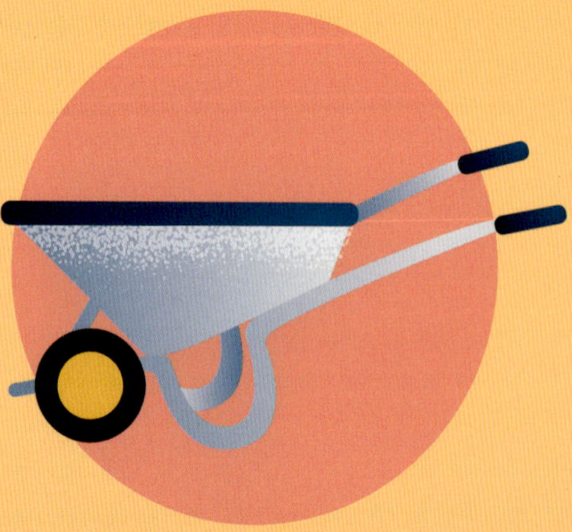

whale, wheat, wheelbarrow, whisk, whisper, whistle

Point to and say the things on this page that start with the /w/ sound. In these words, the /w/ sound is spelled **wh**.

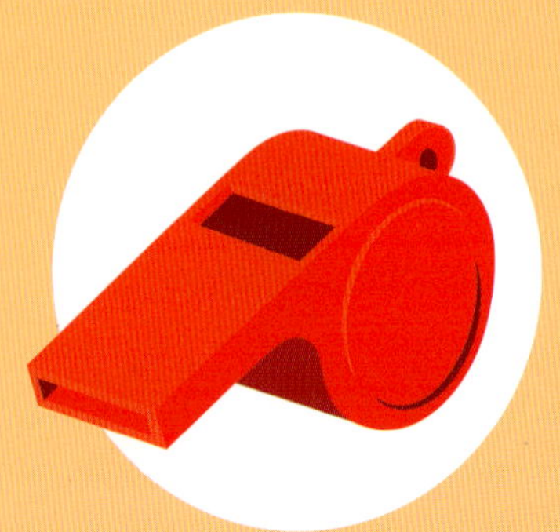

Find and say the 8 things on this page that begin with the /k/ and /w/ sounds blended together. In these words, the /k/ and /w/ sounds are spelled **qu**.

quack, quail, queen, quest, question, quill, quilt, quokka

qu

The sounds /k/ and /w/ together are spelled **qu**. Blend the /k/ and /w/ sounds together to try saying this.

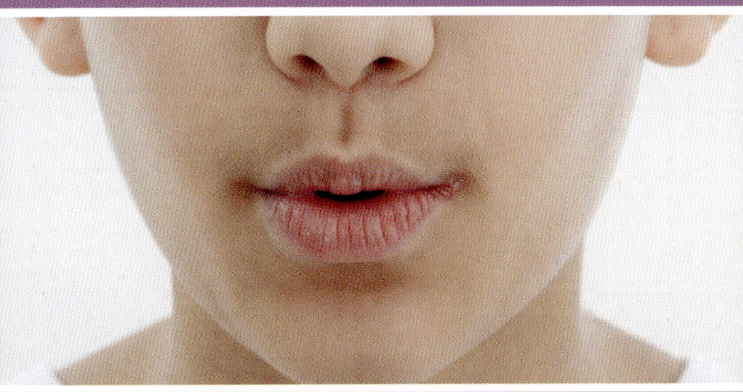

Can you read aloud these words that start with **qu**?

quiz **qu**ick

quilt **qu**est

Would you like to go on quest? Where would you go? What would you do?

ph

The /f/ sound can also be spelled **ph**.

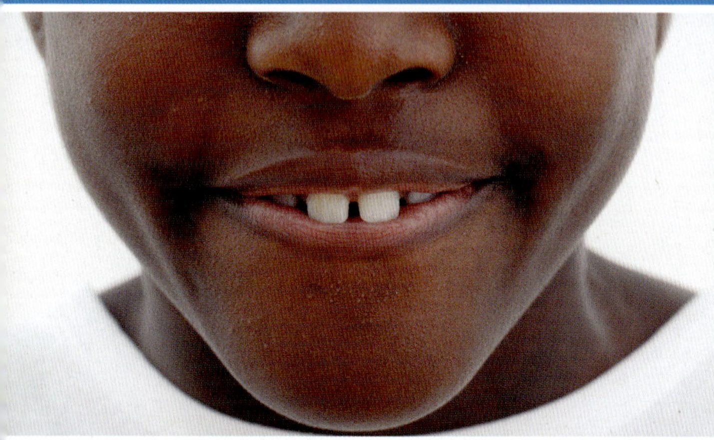

Can you read aloud these words that have **ph** in them?

gra**ph** ele**ph**ant

al**ph**abet dol**ph**in

Phenomenal!

Find and say the 9 things in the picture that have the /f/ sound in them. In these words, the /f/ sound is spelled **ph**.

alphabet, dolphin, elephant, gopher, graph, phone, photo, sphinx, trophy

Find and say the 13 things that end with **le** on this page.

apple, bottle, bubble, cable, candle, cattle, juggle, kettle, puddle, rattle, saddle, stable, table

le

Many two-syllable words end with a consonant and then **le**. Blend the consonant sound, the schwa sound, and the /l/ sound together to make this syllable sound.

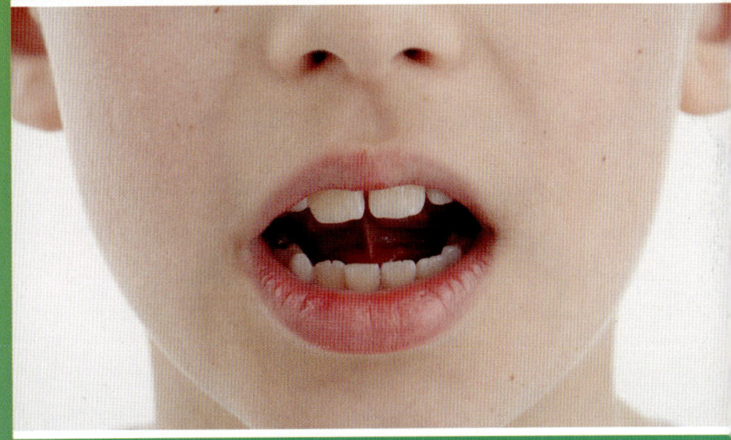

Can you read aloud these words that end in **le**?

middl**e** bottl**e**
handl**e** saddl**e**

What animal lives in a stable?

s, si, ge /zh/

Say the /zh/ sound. There are several ways to spell the /zh/ sound. This page introduces the spellings **s**, **si**, and **ge**.

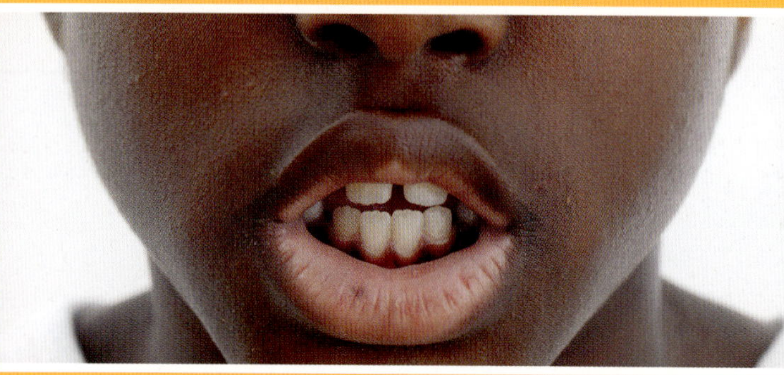

Ask an adult to help you read aloud these words with **s**, **si,** and **ge** in them:

mea**s**ure vi**si**on

trea**s**ure colla**ge**

Which animals camouflage themselves?

beige, camouflage, division, explosion, measure, rouge, television

Can you find the treasure?

Point to and say the other 7 things in this picture that have the /zh/ sound in them.

÷3

a–e

Say the /ai/ sound. The /ai/ sound can be spelled **a–e**. This is when **a** is followed by a consonant and then **e**.

Can you read aloud these words that have **a–e** in them?

name **plate**
same **shape**

Do you like to play games?

Can you find and say the 11 things in the picture that have the /ai/ sound in them. In these words, the /ai/ sound is spelled **a–e**.

cake, cane, cape, cave, game, grapes, milkshake, plane, plate, rake, snake

Point to and say the things on this page that have the /ee/ sound in them. In these words, the /ee/ sound is spelled **e–e**.

e–e

Say the /ee/ sound. The /ee/ sound can be spelled **e–e**. This is when **e** is followed by a consonant and then **e**.

Can you read aloud these words that have **e–e** in them?

theme **delete**

these **compete**

Mission complete!

compete, complete, concrete, delete, trapeze

i-e

Say the /igh/ sound. The /igh/ sound can be spelled **i-e**. This is when **i** is followed by a consonant and then **e**.

Can you read aloud these words that have **i-e** in them?

time	bike
fine	ride

How many bees can you count flying into the hive?

Can you find and say the 14 things in the picture that have the /igh/ sound in them? In these words, the /igh/ sound is spelled **i-e**.

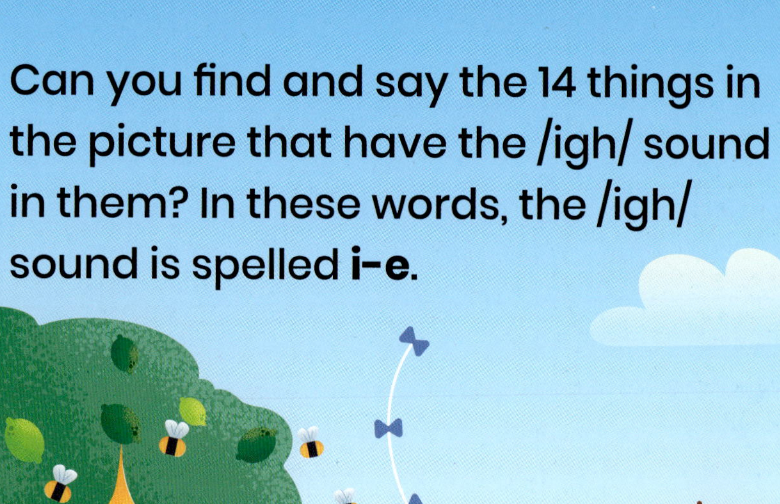

bike, bite, dice, dive, drive, five, hide,
hive, kite, lime, mice, nine, smile, time

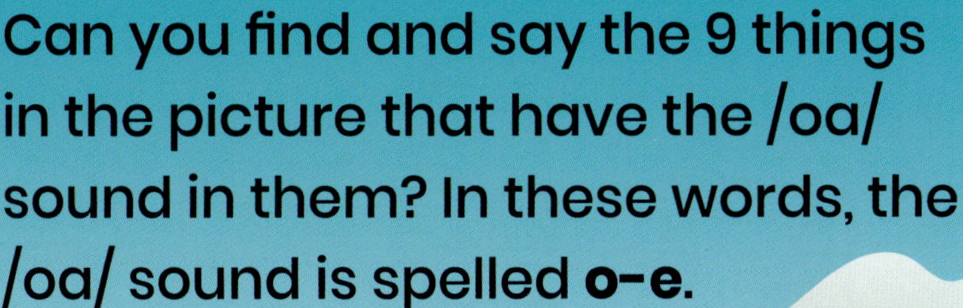

Can you find and say the 9 things in the picture that have the /oa/ sound in them? In these words, the /oa/ sound is spelled **o-e**.

o-e

Say the /oa/ sound.
The /oa/ sound can be spelled **o-e**. This is when **o** is followed by a consonant and then **e**.

Can you read aloud these words that have **o-e** in them?

joke	**slope**
pose	**hope**

You are in the zone!

bone, cone, hose, nose, phone, rope, rose, slope, smoke

u-e /oo/

Say the /oo/ sound. The /oo/ sound can be spelled **u-e**. This is when **u** is followed by a consonant and then **e**.

Can you read aloud these words that have **u-e** in them?

rude	plume
flume	rule

Can you play the flute?

Point to and say the things on this page that have the /oo/ sound in them. In these words, the /oo/ sound is spelled **u-e**.

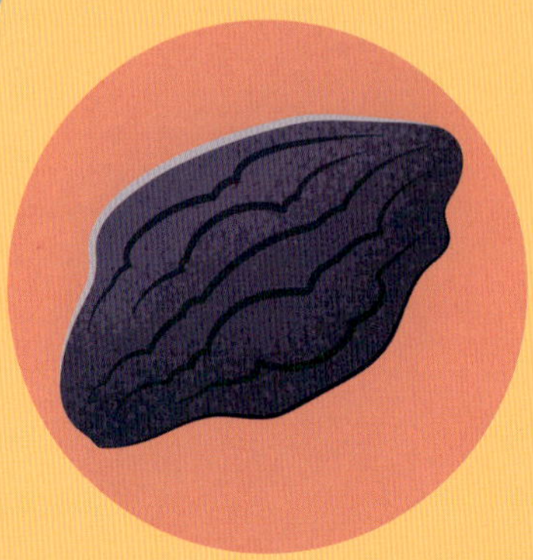

flute, flume, plume, prune, ruler, salute

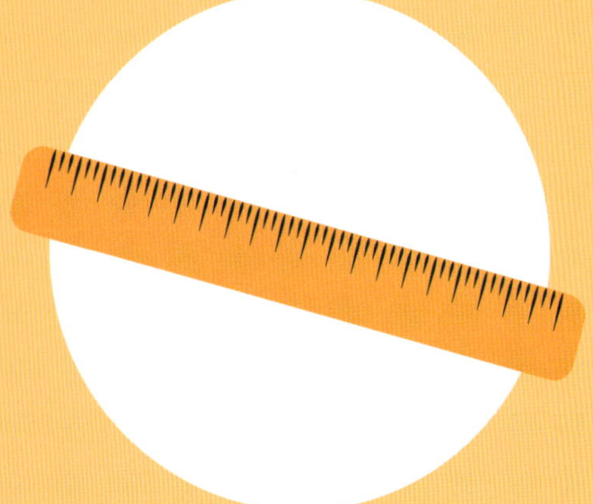

Point to and say the things on this page that have the /ue/ sound in them. In these words, the /ue/ sound is spelled **u-e**.

u-e
/ue/

Say the /ue/ sound. The /ue/ sound can be spelled **u-e**. This is when **u** is followed by a consonant and then **e**.

Can you read aloud these words that have **u-e** in them?

cute	mute
huge	cube

What animals do you think are cute?

cube, fuse, mule, mute

ai, ay, a

Say the /ai/ sound. There are several ways to spell the /ai/ sound. This page introduces the spellings **ai**, **ay**, and **a**.

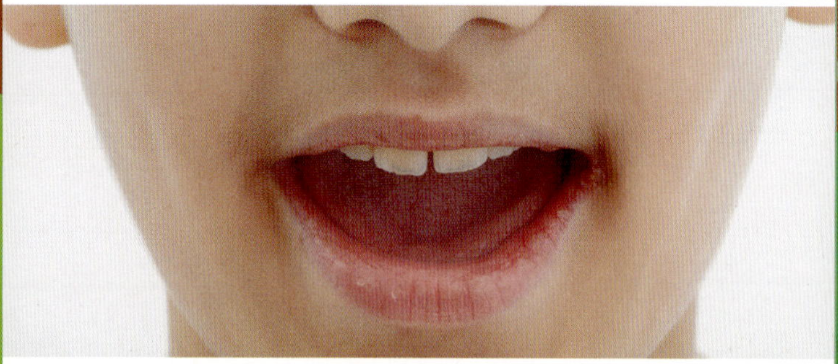

Can you read aloud these words with **ai, ay,** or **a** in them?

hail	may
fail	say
drain	apron
plain	acorn
pay	baby
play	bacon

That is a lot of rain!

Can you find and say the 16 other things in this picture that have the /ai/ sound in them?

Way to go!

bay, cable, chain, drain, hay, mail, nail, paint, rail, railway, sail, snail, stable, table, train, trail

Look it's a peach tree!

Can you find and say the 15 other things in this picture that have the /ee/ sound in them?

ee, ea, e

Say the /ee/ sound. There are several ways to spell the /ee/ sound. This page introduces the spellings **ee**, **ea**, and **e**.

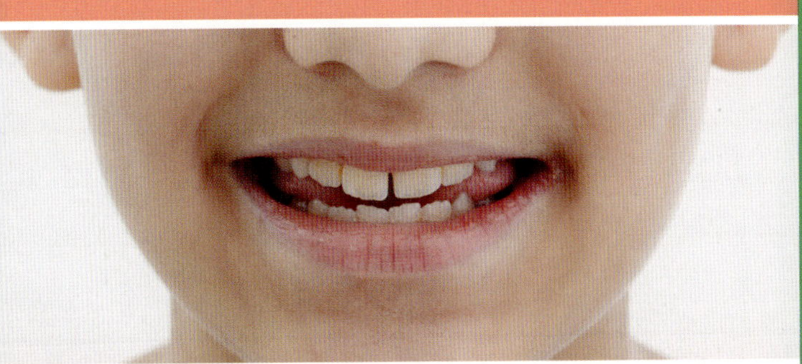

Can you read aloud these words with **ee**, **ea** or **e** in them?

see	heal
feed	me
peel	be
reach	we
leave	she

How many geese can you count on this page?

bee, beet, beetle, cheek, cheese, coffee, equal, geese, leash, pea, queen, read, reed, sheep, team

y, igh, ie, i

Say the /igh/ sound. There are several ways to spell the /igh/ sound. This page introduces the spellings **y**, **igh**, **ie**, and **i**.

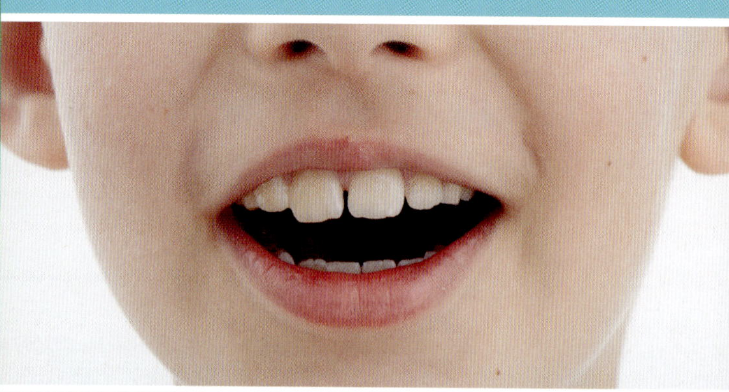

Can you read aloud these words that have **y**, **igh**, **ie**, or **i** in them?

my	**lie**
try	**pie**
high	**hi**
sigh	**idol**

Go on, give it a try!

The teacher had quite a fright!

Can you find and say the 9 other things in this picture that have the /igh/ sound in them?

cry, fight, fries, magpie, pie, shy, sky, spider, tie

oa

Say the /oa/ sound. There are several ways to spell the /oa/ sound. This page introduces the spellings **oa**, **ow**, and **o**.

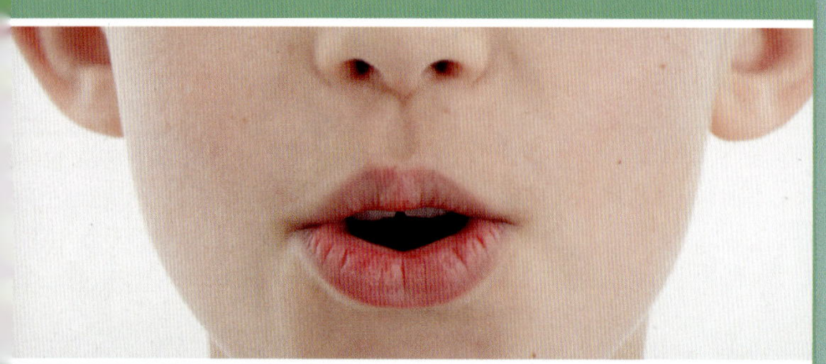

Can you read aloud these words that have **oa**, **ow**, or **o** in them?

load	low
foam	go
moat	so
bow	no

What type of building often has a moat?

Go, go, go!

Point to and say the 16 things that have the /oa/ sound in them in the pictures below.

banjo, blow, boat, crow, goat, grow, hero, moat, piano, pony, throw, toad, toast, row, snow, soap

ar

Say the /ar/ sound.

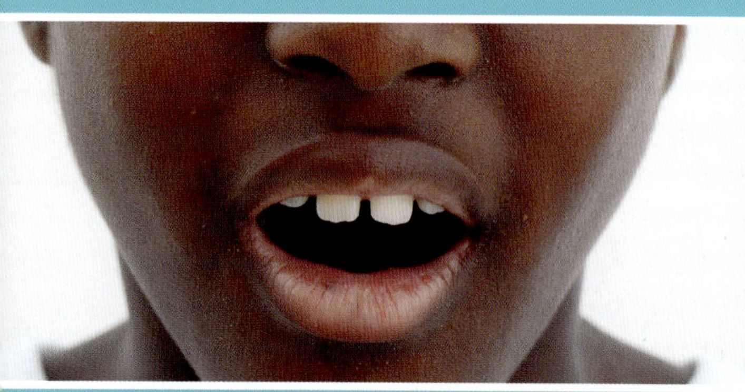

Can you read aloud these words with **ar** in?

mark	yard
dark	car

Point to and say the things on this page that have the /ar/ sound in them.

art, harp, jar, scarf, shark, star

Point to and say the things on this page that have **or** in them.

or

Many words have **or** in them. Blend the /o/ and /r/ sounds together to try saying this.

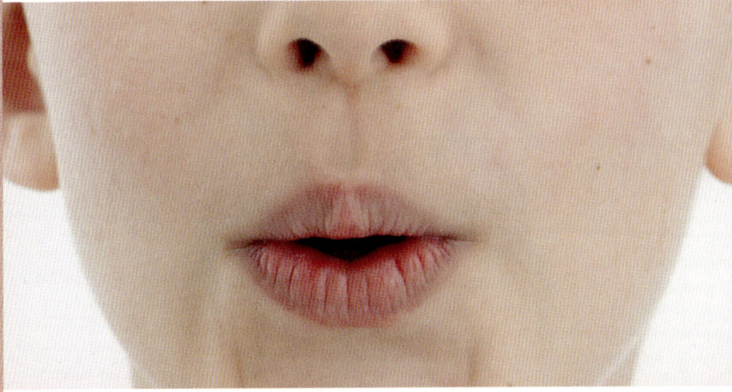

Can you read aloud these words with **or** in?

b**or**n	sh**or**t
n**or**th	p**or**ch

Do you like horses?

corn, fork, horn, north, stork, torch

oo

Say the long /oo/ sound. There are several ways to spell the /oo/ sound. This page introduces the spellings **oo** and **ew**.

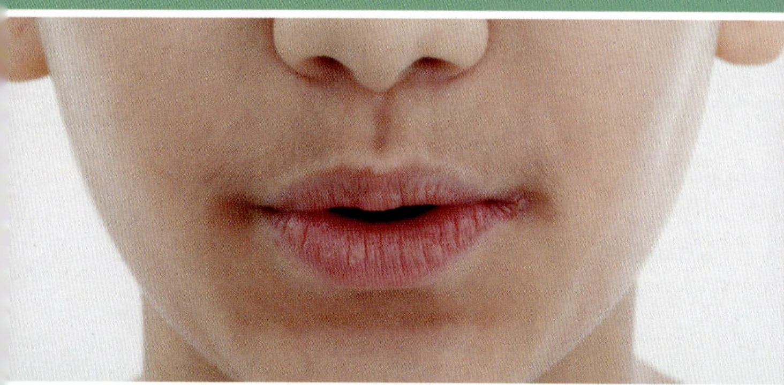

Can you read aloud these words that have **oo** and **ew** in them?

soon	chew
hoop	grew
food	crew

Would you like to fly in a hot-air balloon?

Find and say the 9 things in the picture that have the long /oo/ sound in them.

broom, goose, hoop, hot-air balloon, igloo, moon, moose, screw, shrew

Find and say the 5 things in the picture that have the /ue/ sound in them. In these words, the /ue/ sound is spelled **u**.

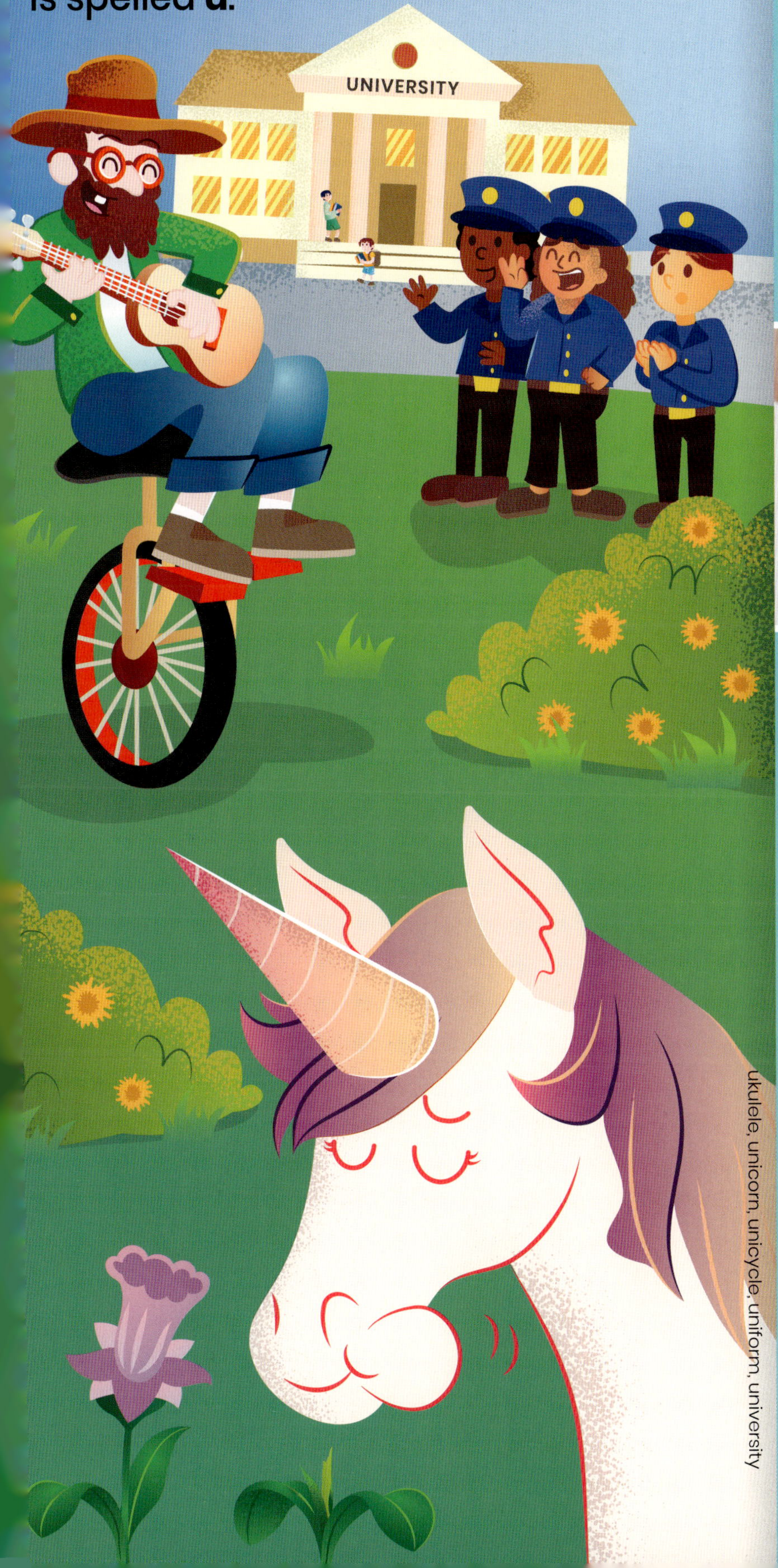

ukulele, unicorn, unicycle, uniform, university

ue

Say the /ue/ sound.
The /ue/ sound can be spelled **u**.

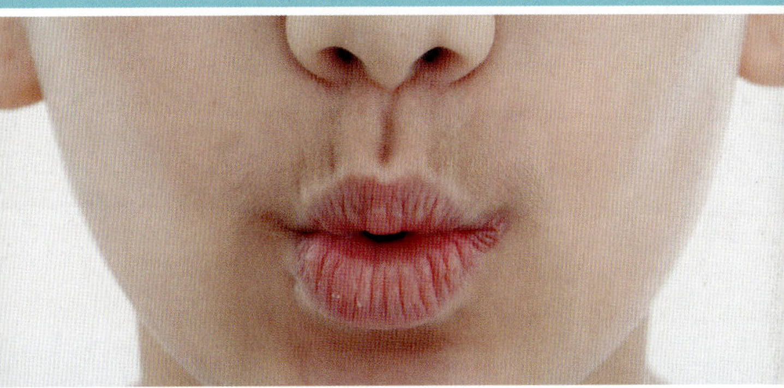

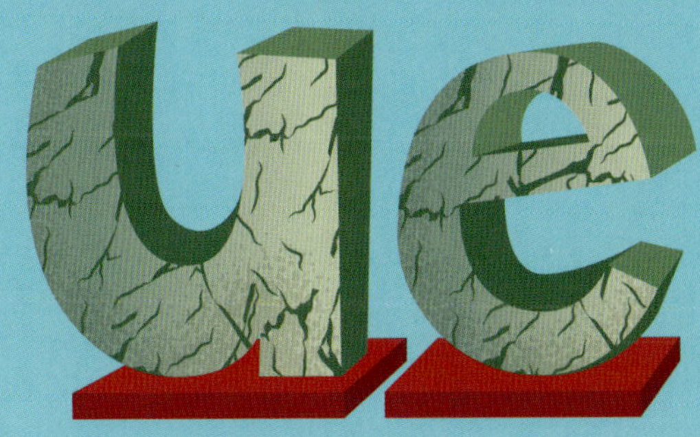

Can you read aloud these words that have **u** in them?

cucumber **music**

unicorn **unit**

Have you ever played a ukulele?

oo

Say the short /oo/ sound.

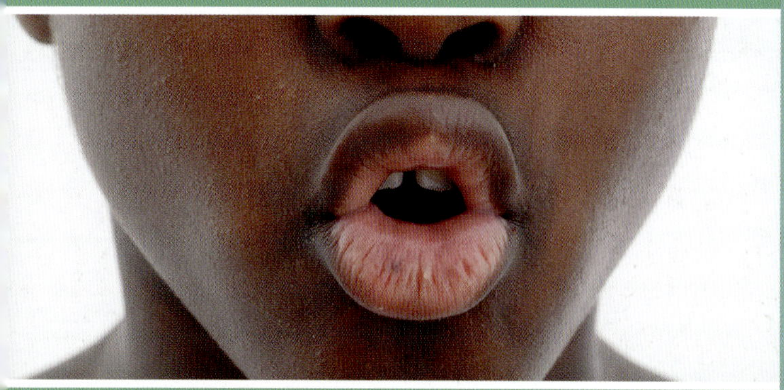

Can you read aloud these words with **oo** in them?

book	**hood**
took	**shook**

What book do you like to read?

Point to and say the things on this page that have the short /oo/ sound in them.

book, hood, hook, look, wood, wool

Point to and say the things on this page that have the /n/ sound in them. In these words, the /n/ sound is spelled **gn**.

gn

The /n/ sound can also be spelled **gn**.

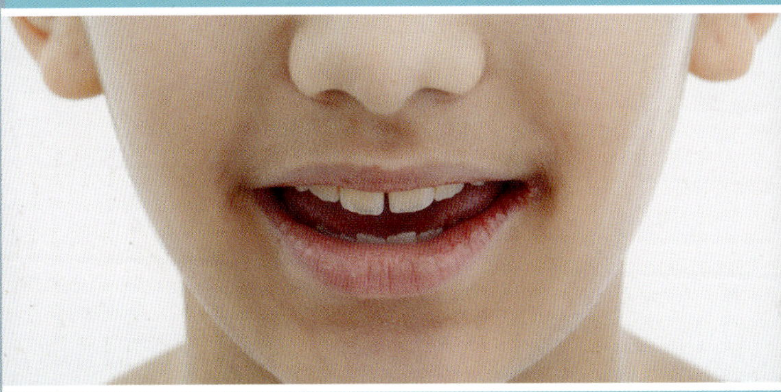

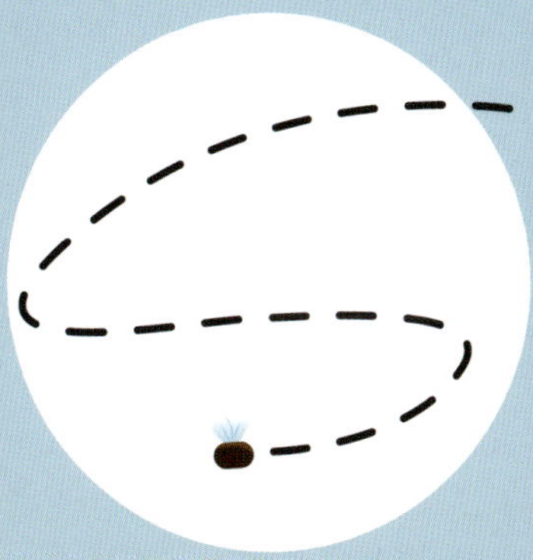

Can you read aloud these words with **gn** in them?

gnash **gn**ome

si**gn** desi**gn**

Your reading reigns supreme!

design, gnat, gnaw, gnome, reign, sign

mb

The /m/ sound can also be spelled **mb.**

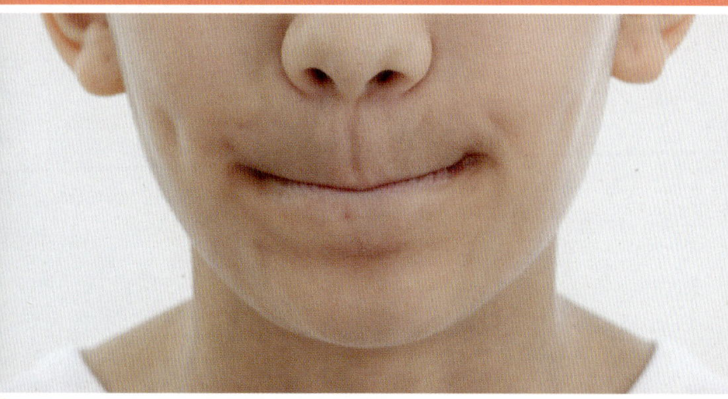

Find and say the 5 things on this page that have the /m/ sound in them. In these words, the /m/ sound is spelled **mb**.

Can you read aloud these words that have **mb** in them?

cli**mb** nu**mb**
li**mb** cru**mb**

The suffix **-er** can be added to base words that end with **-mb**, as in “plumber”.

Thumbs up!

climb, comb, lamb, plumber, thumb

Find and say the 6 things on this page that have the /n/ sound in them. In these words, the /n/ sound is spelled **kn**.

kn

The /n/ sound can also be spelled **kn**.

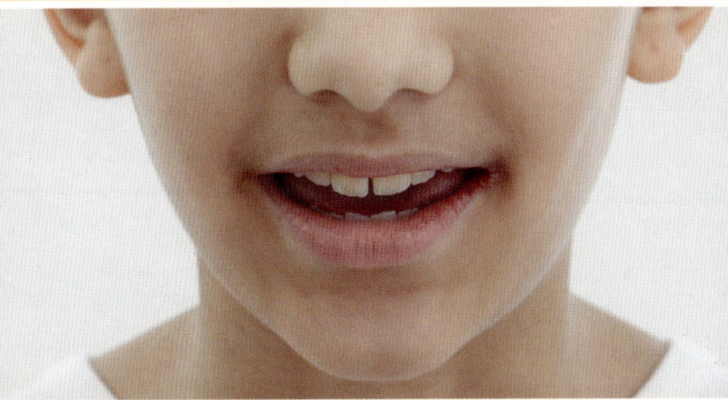

Can you read aloud these words that have **kn** in them?

knight	**knot**
knee	**knit**

You really know your stuff!

knee, knight, knit, knock, knot, knuckle

wr

The /r/ sound can also be spelled **wr**.

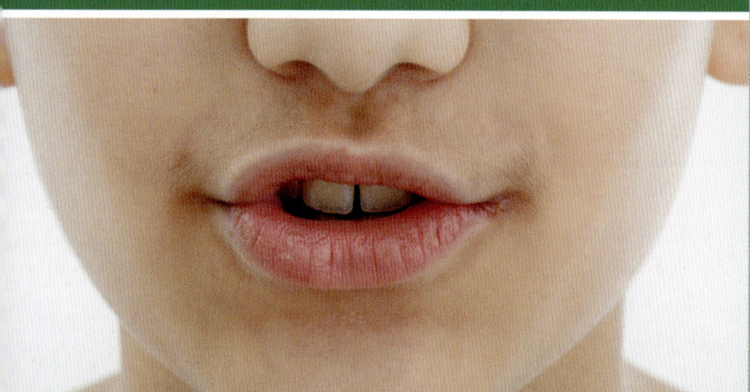

Can you read aloud these words that start with **wr**?

wrong **wr**ite
wreck **wr**ist

Did you know? Words that begin with **wr** usually refer to things that twist or distort.

Point to and say the things on this page that have the /r/ sound in them. In these words, the /r/ sound is spelled **wr.**

wrap, wreath, wreck, wriggle, wrist, write

Point to and say the things on this page that have the /s/ sound in them. In these words, the /s/ sound is spelled **st**.

The /s/ sound can also be spelled **st**.

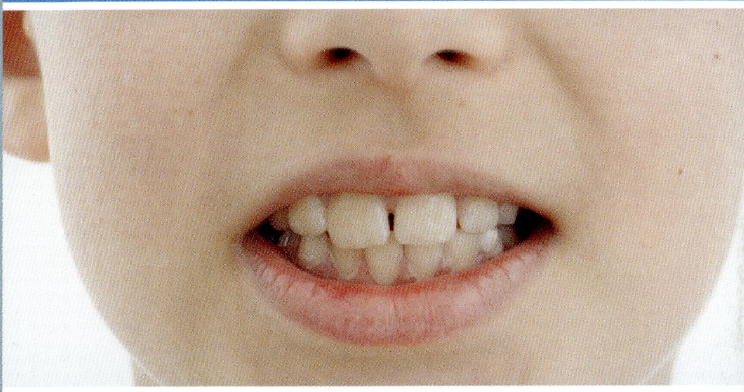

Can you read aloud these words that have **st** in them?

li**st**en	fa**st**en
gli**st**en	ca**st**le

Who might live in a castle?

castle, fasten, listen, thistle, whistle

schwa

A schwa sound is a "lazy" vowel sound in a syllable that is not stressed. It sounds like a clipped /u/ or /i/ and can be represented by any written vowel.

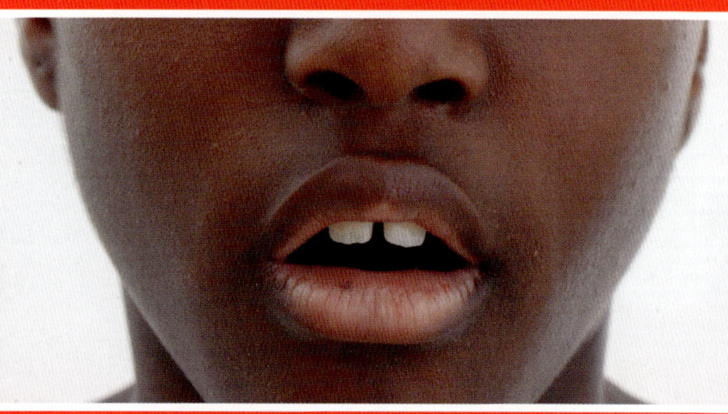

Can you read aloud these words with the **schwa** sound in them?

cam**e**l problem
alone pand**a**

Magical!

Is that gorilla eating a lemon?

Find and say the 14 other things in the picture that have the schwa sound in them.

actor, banana, brother, button, dinosaur, magnet, mitten, panda, parrot, pasta, poster, salad, theater, zebra

aw

Say the /aw/ sound.

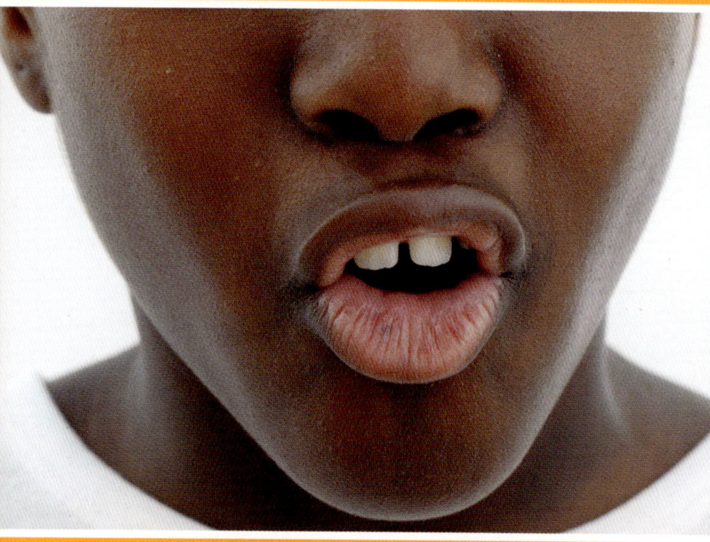

Can you read aloud these words with **aw** in them?

jaw	crawl
saw	yawn

Do you like to draw?

Look at that crab's claw!

Point to the 9 other things in this picture that have the /aw/ sound in them.

draw, hawk, lawn, outlaw, paw, saw, shawl, straw, yawn

Is that surfer holding a burger?

Find and say the 11 other things in this picture that have the /ir/ sound in them.

er, ur, ir

There are several ways to spell the /ir/ sound. This page introduces the spellings **er**, **ur**, and **ir**.

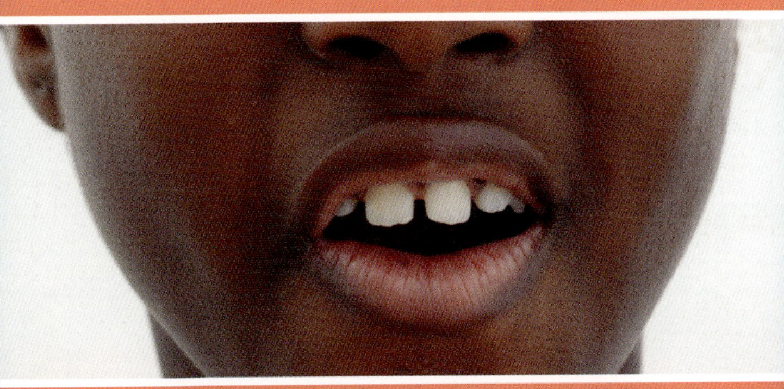

Can you read aloud these words that have **er, ur,** or **ir** in them?

first	church
swirl	turn
fir	her
birthday	verb
hurt	herd
burst	germ

Have you ever been surfing?

bird, burst, church, girl, mermaid, nurse, purple, purse, shirt, skirt, turtle

air, are

Say the /air/ sound. There are several ways to spell the /air/ sound. This page introduces the spellings **air** and **are.**

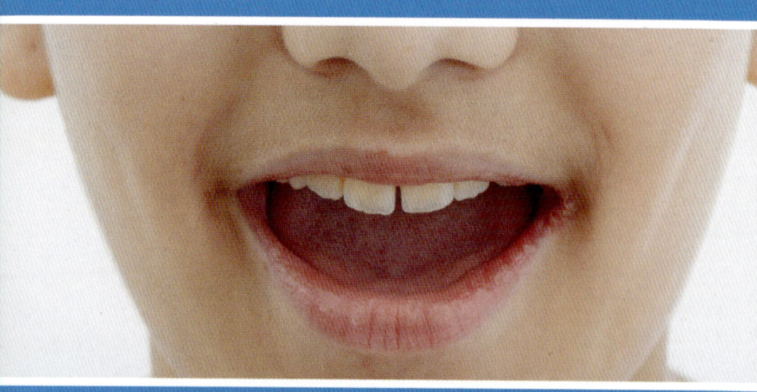

Can you read aloud these words with **air** or **are** in them?

air	bare
lair	glare
pair	fare
chair	dare

Can you name some things that come in pairs?

Look! It's a fair!

Can you find and say the 10 other things in this picture that have the /air/ sound in them?

chair, éclair, fairy, fare, hair, hare, pair, scarecrow, square, stare

ow, ou

Say the /ow/ sound. There are several ways to spell the /ow/ sound. This page introduces the spellings **ow** or **ou.**

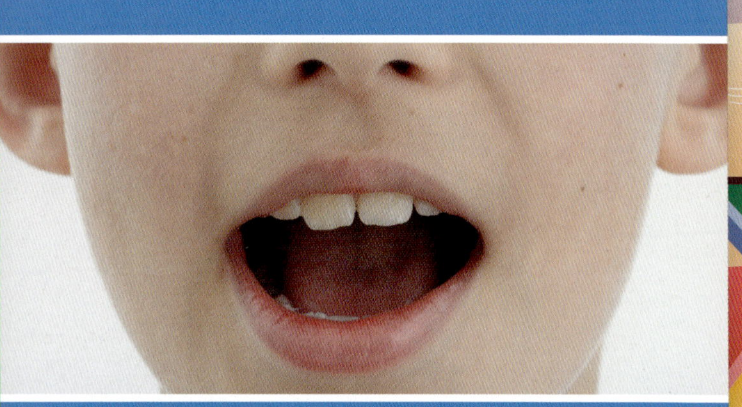

Can you read aloud these words that have **ow** or **ou** in them?

d**ow**n	s**ou**nd
br**ow**n	h**ou**nd
gr**ow**l	c**ou**ch
t**ow**n	m**ou**th

How many people can you count in the crowd?

The wolf can howl loudly!

Can you find and say the 12 other things in this picture that have the /ow/ sound in them?

couch, crowd, crown, frown, gown, hound, house, mouse, mouth, owl, sound, town

oy, oi

Say the /oy/ sound. The /oy/ sound can be spelled **oy** or **oi**. The **oy** spelling typically comes at the end of a word, and the **oi** spelling is usually used in the middle of a word.

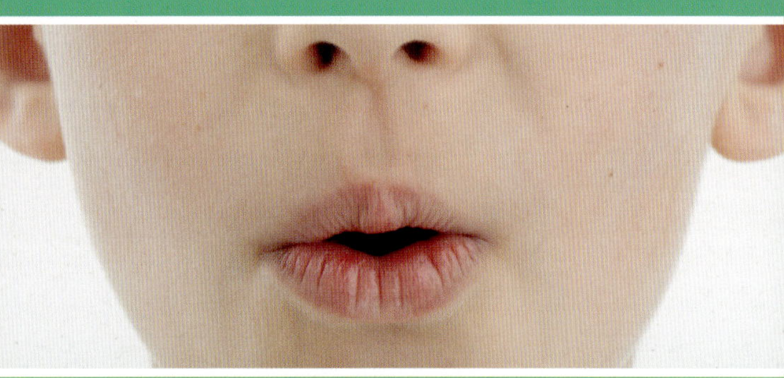

Can you read aloud these words that have **oy** or **oi** in them?

ann**oy**	j**oi**nt
enj**oy**	b**oi**l
b**oy**	h**oi**st
t**oy**	f**oi**l

The cat has lots of coins!

Can you find and say the 9 other things in the picture that have the /oy/ sound in them?

boil, boy, cowboy, noise, oil, oyster, soil, toilet, toy

Which toy do you enjoy playing with?

OIL
OYSTERS

ear, eer

Say the /ear/ sound. There are several ways to spell the /ear/ sound. This page introduces the spellings **ear** and **eer**.

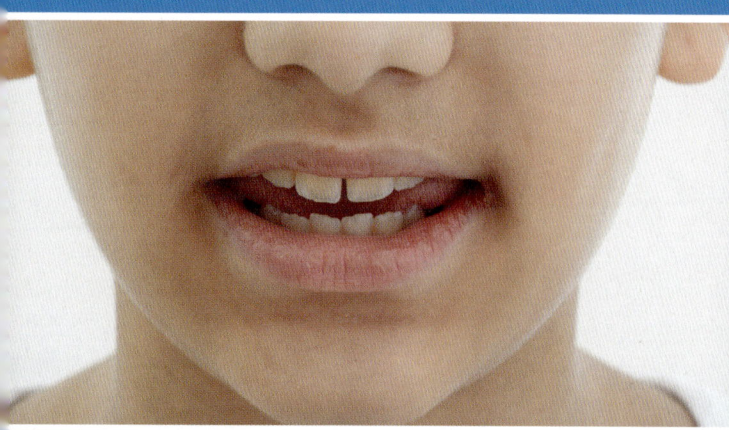

Can you read aloud these words that have **ear** or **eer** in them?

hear	**deer**
tear	**steer**

Find and say the 7 things in the picture that have the /ear/ sound in them.

beard, cheer, deer, ear, hear, meerkat, steer

Hooray! You deserve a big cheer!

Point to and say the things on this page that have the /ure/ sound in them.

cure, impure, pure, secure

ure

Say the /ure/ sound. This sound is often spelled **ure**.

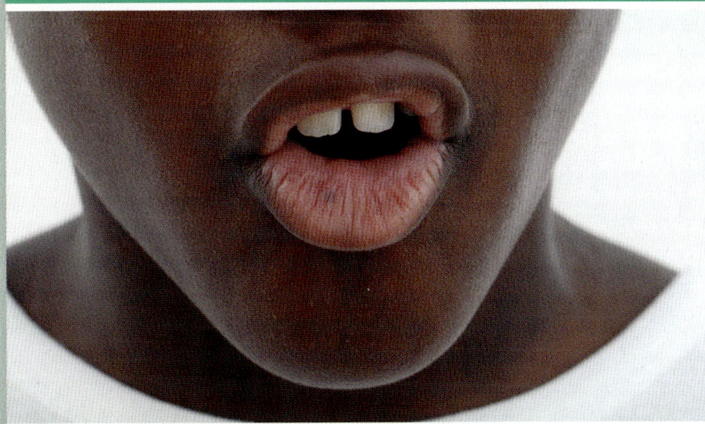

Ask an adult to help you read aloud these words with **ure** in them:

imp**ure** sec**ure**

p**ure** c**ure**

Can you spot the pure and impure water?

When there is more than one of something, often **s** will be added to the end of the word. In these words, **s** can spell the /s/ sound or the /z/ sound.

Can you read aloud these words that end in **s**?

hats	dogs
rats	pens

How many cats can you count in the picture?

balloons, bananas, books, cats

Point to and say the things that end with **s** on this page. Do they end in the /s/ sound or the /z/ sound?

Point to and say the things that end in **es** on this page.

When there is more than one of something, sometimes **es** will be added to the end of the word. Blend the /i/ and /z/ sounds together to try saying this.

Can you read aloud these words that end in **es**?

buses **kisses**

boxes **sashes**

Do you like peaches?

boxes, buses, matches, peaches, prizes, watches

-ies

When there is more than one of something that ends with a consonant followed by a **y**, the **y** is removed and replaced by **ies** at the end of the word. Blend the /ee/ and /z/ sounds together to try saying this.

Can you read aloud these words that end in **ies**?

puppies parties
bunnies fairies

How many bunnies can you count in the picture?

babies, bunnies, cherries, cities,
parties, ponies, puppies

Find and say the 7 things ending with **ies** in the picture.

Point to and say the things on this page that end in **ly**.

-ly

Many words end in **ly** to show how something is done. Blend the /l/ and /ee/ sounds together to try saying this.

Can you read aloud these words that end in **ly**?

sad**ly** quick**ly**
bad**ly** glad**ly**

Say the words slowly, then quickly.

happily, loudly, quickly, quietly, sadly, slowly

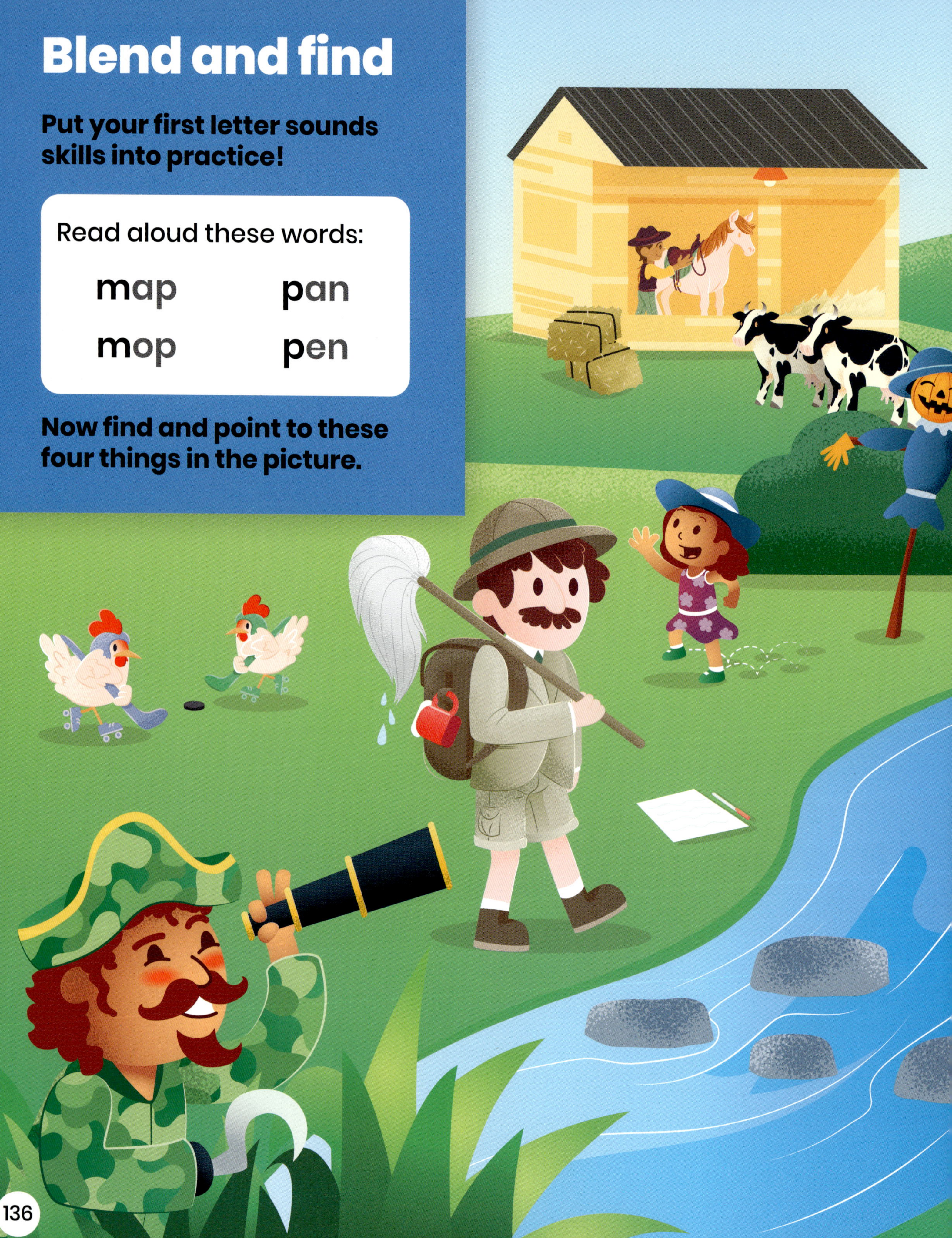

Blend and find

Put your first letter sounds skills into practice!

Read aloud these words:

map **pan**
mop **pen**

Now find and point to these four things in the picture.

Blend and find

Check your knowledge of consonant digraphs!

Read aloud these words:

ship	chick
fish	chess

Now find and point to these things in the picture.

Blend and find

See how much you know about vowel spellings!

Read aloud these words:

train	tree
mail	bee

Now find and point to these things in the picture.

Glossary

accuracy
Reading words without making any mistakes.

advanced or extended code
The sounds and graphemes that are taught later in a phonics program once the basics have been established. This deals with more complex aspects of the code.

basic or initial code
The sounds and letters taught at the beginning of a phonics program where the child is given the impression that each sound is represented by just one single letter.

blending
The ability to "push" sounds together or combine them to make a spoken word. When reading a word, children look at the graphemes, say the sounds, and blend the sounds together to read the word.

CVC word
A word with three sounds, made up of a consonant, vowel, consonant, e.g., "hug" and "pug."

CVCC word
A word with four sounds in, made up of a consonant, vowel, consonant, consonant, e.g., "camp" or "tent."

CCVC word
A word with four sounds in, made up of a consonant, consonant, vowel, consonant, e.g., "flag" or "drop."

CCVCC word
A word with five sounds in, made up of a consonant, consonant, vowel, consonant, consonant, e.g., "skunk" or "stamp."

code knowledge
What the child knows about the sounds of the alphabet and the graphemes that represent them.

consonant
A sound produced with the air flow from the mouth at least partially stopped, e.g., /d/ /n/ /s/.

digraph
A grapheme (combination of letters) that is made up of two letters.

fluency
Reading with good pace and expression so it sounds natural.

grapheme
A letter or combination of letters that represent a sound (phoneme).

letter formation
The act of writing a letter, forming a letter shape using a pen or pencil.

long vowel
A vowel that is longer in duration when spoken, e.g., /ai/ /ee/ /ie/ /oa/ /ue/ /oo/.

phoneme
The smallest unit of sound in a spoken word. Spoken words are made up of these phonemes.

phonics
A body of knowledge about the correspondences between sounds and letters. This includes some key skills—blending (for reading) and segmenting (for spelling)—and the understanding of some simple concepts about how written language works.

schwa
An "uh" sound spoken in place of a predictable vowel sound in a multisyllable word to make the flow of speaking easier.

short vowel
A vowel that is shorter in duration when spoken, e.g., /a/ /e/ /i/ /o/ /u/.

sounds of the alphabet
The way that the 44 sounds (phonemes) are represented by graphemes (letters and letter combinations). This is sometimes described as a "code" that uses the alphabet.

syllable
A group of sounds in a word that are spoken as a "beat" in natural speech and must include a vowel.

tetragraph
A grapheme (combination of letters) that is made up of four letters.

trigraph
A grapheme (combination of letters) that is made up of three letters.

unvoiced sounds
Sounds produced by the movement of air passing through open vocal cords with no vibration of the cords. Children cannot feel a vibration as they say the sounds *(see voiced sounds)*.

visual mnemonic
A picture that helps a child to remember the shape of the letter and the sound it represents.

voiced sounds
Sounds produced when air passes through the vocal cords causing them to vibrate to make the sound. Children can feel the vibration as they say the sound *(see unvoiced sounds)*.

vowel
A sound produced with the mouth relaxed and open allowing a free outflow of air, e.g., /a/ /i/ /oo/ /oa/.

Produced for DK by Collaborate Agency
Introduction and glossary by Ann Sullivan
Illustrated by Eugenia Ferrer, Melany Lerda Olberg, Victoria Murzi, and Andrés Vaisberg

Publisher Sarah Forbes
Managing Editor Katherine Neep
Managing Art Editor Sarah Corcoran
Senior Art Editor Gilda Pacitti
Project Editor Sophie Adam
Editor Bryony Brain
Production Editor Sachin Gupta
Production Controller Isabell Schart

First American Edition, 2025
Published in the United States by DK Publishing, a division of Penguin Random House LLC
1745 Broadway, 20th Floor, New York, NY 10019

25 26 27 28 29 10 9 8 7 6 5 4 3 2 1
001–344572–Jan/2025

Published in Great Britain by Dorling Kindersley Limited

A catalog record for this book is available from the Library of Congress.
ISBN: 978-0-5939-5879-7

Printed and bound in China

www.dk.com

This book was made with Forest Stewardship Council™ certified paper – one small step in DK's commitment to a sustainable future.
Learn more at www.dk.com/uk/information/sustainability